Being Single to be Ma

Copyright © 2012, JA Publishing

The right of Jacqueline Nwokeji-Ani to be identified as the author of this book has been asserted in accordance with the Copyright, Designs and Patents Act 1988.

First Edition published in 2012 by JA Publishing Company Ltd

JA Publishing Company

info@jainspirationalspeaker.com

www.jainspirationalspeaker.com

Ordering Information: Quantity sales are available for corporations, associations, and others. For details, contact the publisher at the email address above.

International Standard Book Number: ISBN 978-0-9548340-1-2

Scripture quotations marked (NLT) are taken from the Holy Bible, New Living Translation, copyright © 1996, 2004, 2007 by Tyndale House Foundation. Used by permission of Tyndale House Publishers, Inc., Carol Stream, Illinois 60188. All rights reserved.

Scripture quotations marked (AMP) are taken from the Amplified® Bible, Copyright © 1954, 1958, 1962, 1964, 1965, 1987 by The Lockman Foundation. Used by permission. (www.Lockman.org)

Unless marked otherwise, all other scriptures are quoted from the New King James Version © 1982 of the Holy Bible by Thomas Nelson, Inc. All rights reserved.

Brand and product names are trademarks of registered trademarks of their respective owners. Cover designed by Purple Rose Design. Typeset by Loud Voice Publishing, division of Loud Voice Communications Ltd

Printed in the United Kingdom

Being Single to be Married

A GUIDE TO PREPARING YOURSELF FOR A PURPOSE DRIVEN MARRIAGE

For the Single and the Married

BY JACQUELINE NWOKEJI-ANI

About the Author

Jacqueline Nwokeji-Ani is an inspirational speaker, author, prophetic mentor, life strategist and social entrepreneur.

Her career started when she made the choice, after her undergraduate degree, to go into human resources and recruitment and selection. Recruiting for triple A rated investment banks in the City of London, Jacqueline was one of the most successful Temp Recruitment Consultants working for a renowned search and selection outfit in the City.

Realising that the industry was a thriving one, she set out to start her own recruitment consultancy, where she recruited management personnel for blue chip organisations. This is where she discovered her calling in writing and encouraging women to move beyond their limitations with their abilities and not allowing circumstances hold them back.

With this in mind, she retrained as an adult literacy lecturer delivering programmes to support adults back into employment. Jacqueline Nwokeji-Ani is the Founder of Empowered Woman Ltd, The Mentoring Academy and Jacqueline Ani Inspirational Speaker. She is married with two beautiful girls. She has also written two other books—'*The Widow's Jar of Oil*' and '*Your Talent is Your Wealth*'.

Acknowledgments

To the man whose vision I am and who has given me the opportunity to complete this book—Mr Frank Ani, my companion, friend, husband, lover, brother and inspiration.

May you always continue to excel in everything you put your hands to do, and be the man who is always after God's heart.

To my two beautiful daughters, who even before I knew them, I thought of and envisioned in appearance. You are precious to both of us and I know that you are empowered women in the making.

To the inspiration behind me, my resources, my gifts and blessings—The Holy Spirit. Continue to keep my eyes and my heart stayed on You.

Contents

INTRODUCTION - 10

CHAPTER 1 – LIVING SINGLE AND BEING WHOLE - 15

CHAPTER 2 – THE EVIDENCE OF DESIRE IS PURSUIT - 25

CHAPTER 3 – KNOWING YOUR PURPOSE - 37
Your destiny has already been planned - 38
Katherine Khulman's Mission - 39
A Wife for Isaac—The Story of Abraham, Isaac, Rebekah and Eliazar 45
Eliazar discovers Rebekah - 48
The qualities of a potentially good wife - 52
Making the right choice - 58
Reflection Time - 62

CHAPTER 4 – A WOMAN'S POWER IS IN SUBMITTING THE RIGHT WAY - 63
Rebekah submits to the promise - 66
The real pearls - 57
If you love someone, set them free - 69
The day I met him - 74
The grace to submit to God - 76
Submitting the right way - 78
Submitting the wrong way - 82
Testimonies of women who submitted the right way - 84
How Rebekah's role depicted fulfilling purpose - 86
Reflection Time Case Study - 88

CHAPTER 5 – MEN NEED THEIR OWN REVELATION TO LOVE - 89
Major events can change your focus - 93
Relocating for purpose - 96
The epitome of his vision - 98
He can only love when he knows God's Love - 100
How Isaac's role depicted fulfilling purpose - 103
Reflection Time Case Study - 105

CHAPTER 6 – BE READY, GET INTO POSITION AND RECEIVE - 107
There is provision for every need - 110
What does it mean to be in position? - 114
Walking in obedience - 121
And it came to pass… receive the promise - 123
Reflection Time - 126

CHAPTER 7 –THE PURPOSE DRIVEN MARRIAGE - 127
What is a purpose driven marriage? - 129
Is divorce a problem or symptom? - 130
The first true male and female - 132
The first true male man - 133
Qualities of the first true male man - 134
The first true female woman - 135
Qualities of the first true female woman - 136
God's model design for a purpose driven marriage - 138
The art of marital bliss - 140
Reflection - 143

AUTHOR'S CONCLUSION - 144

The Lord will hold you in His Hand for all to see
A splendid crown in the Hand of God
Never again will you be called "The Forsaken
City" or the "Desolate Land"
Your new name will be called "The City of God's
Delight"
And "The Bride of God"
For the Lord delights in you as His bride.

Isaiah 62: 3-4 NLT

BEING SINGLE TO BE MARRIED

Introduction

0

Introduction

WHEN I was a teenager, I remember my aunties, who were then in their mid to late 30's and sometimes 40's, visiting us to talk to my mother for some motherly advice; they were looking for explanations and answers as to why at their mature age they were still not married. Their biological clocks were ticking and they couldn't understand what was delaying their opportunity to get engaged and walk down the aisle to exchange wedding vows.

At that early time in my life, I couldn't understand what the big issue was about. I remember thinking to myself that it could be their own fault as to why they were still single. 'May be they did something wrong. May be they were too promiscuous, that's why they hadn't found husbands. If my aunt made an effort with her appearance, then perhaps she would attract the right man.' My attitude towards them was that of indifference. After all, I didn't know what the big deal was.

By my mid 20's, I had already planned my special day in my mind. I had planned that by the age of 28, I would meet my handsome 'knight in shining armour' and prepare for the wedding ceremony of the century. I would live in a big house with a cat and a dog (children did not come into my dream) and we would both have wonderful careers and travel the world together. How exciting!

Instead, at the age of 36, I saw myself living my aunties' predicaments: in my mid 30's, still single and my dream wedding ceremony reduced to an illusionary fairy tale. Whilst I am not disputing that you can meet the man of your dreams and have a successful marriage later in life, the dream turns to reality and maturity prepares you for the knight in shining armour who may have issues of his own and is not looking to come and rescue his damsel who may be in distress with tons of emotional baggage.

If you want a partner who is whole, then you as a singleton need to spend the time on yourself to learn how to be a whole individual. The most important experience I have had in my journey as a single woman into marriage came from my knowledge and experience as a Christian. Christ helped me develop a relationship with my Creator – God. If not for Him, I don't know who I would be yoked with today.

I am happy to say that maturity and reality has removed the illusions I had about meeting and marrying my life partner and my deep desire to be married taught me how to discover my destiny; to know who I am and what I have in my possession before I could be a wife to any man.

The revelation in this book is to bring truth to remove the illusions, to introduce light where darkness has dwelt, and to bring understanding to those looking for knowledge in this area. First, it is important to understand that God created and ordained the principles for a good marriage. He instructed that we should live it the way Christ lives with the Church.

Marriage is a ministry and the role of wife and husband is a calling to that ministry. In the same way that pastors are called to preach, evangelists are called to evangelise, doctors are called to heal and teachers are called to teach, so a wife and husband are called to the ministry of marriage. In the same way God trains us to walk in those callings, He also trains us during our seasons of singlehood to discover our potential in Him to create and build a purpose driven marriage; to be united together as one to effectively serve each other, build a family and community, and promote His Kingdom.

Sometimes we make mistakes and even get marriage wrong – but if we believe that marriage should be and is a blessing, then we should allow the Holy Spirit to guide, direct and teach us how to walk into it and stay in it. That means dying to ourselves.

Today, I believe that yielding myself to what I needed to learn in my season of singlehood taught me God's intended will for marriage, why He has called some of us to be married, and the need to fulfil His destiny on earth as married people. After all, the bible says that one can put a thousand to flight but two can put ten thousand to flight. The institution of marriage should be a joy because it is a blessing from God and whatever is a good and perfect (free, large, full) gift is from above. It comes down from the Father of (that gives) light. He never changes or casts a shifting shadow (James 1:17 NLT).

Before one can successfully embark on marriage, it is very important to understand why we were created as single people and the opportunity the single season teaches us. I have often asked myself why God didn't create us already married. It would have made a lot of sense. That way we could come into the world already married to someone and without having to deal with the issues that relationships can sometimes bring. However, God knew what He was doing when He first made us an individual male and female before He made us husbands and wives.

When I started writing this book, I was unmarried. I desired to be married, but now understand I had to go through the process of knowing who I am and how I can be a helper to my husband when he finds me. Six years on I am happily married to a wonderful man. I've always wanted to love my husband in the good and the difficult times, have children and have all the pleasures that marriage brings. It took me 10 years to understand why being single was an important stage in my life. I understood the importance of discovering who I am and why I was created at this time. Having faith in something that I couldn't comprehend would happen has a lot to do with where I am today.

The relationship helped me discover who I am and how to bring this experience to the table of marriage. My illusions then and the reality of marriage now means that it is not always an easy ride, but the principles I learnt during my single season has prepared me to be a wife prepared by God for my husband, although there is still more for me to learn as a married woman. We must learn to live and enjoy being single before we can ever think of serving a mate in our roles as wife or husband, or else we could end up living an unhappy married life. At the same time I also believe that if you desire to be married, there is an appointed time where God will meet your need and your role is to ensure that you are prepared for that time and not let it pass you by. I encourage you to embrace your single season but also look forward to moving on when it is time.

When I was single, once in awhile I would ask my married friends how their relationships were going. Depending on the times and seasons their relationships were going through, I got different replies such as, 'It's tough' or 'It's wonderful'! However, whatever storm you find your relationship in, I really believe that your positive experiences of living single will always help you ride the storm as they come when you're married.

This book has been written for those who have been expectantly waiting to be married, to help you know how to wait in the appropriate way as a single person until you meet your mate, as well as what to prepare for so you can say 'I do' with an element of understanding about what you are getting into. Marriage is a good thing and there are wonderful benefits to being married. But there are also wonderful benefits to being single, and until you can understand and appreciate YOUR ESSENCE, making a journey down the aisle will be futile.

It has also been written for those who are already married and believe that even though they may not be enjoying the benefits of marriage, it is still possible to move beyond a mediocre relationship with their spouse to living in purpose in their marriage. God still loves them and wants them to know and understand His Principles of marriage so that they can apply it and see transformation in themselves and essentially their marriage.

My desire is that when you read this book and study the principles of the Kingdom and apply it as a medication to the areas of your marriage that need healing, it will do what the Word says it will do. The only one that loves divorce is the adversary. When a marriage breaks down, don't think about those who made the decision to go that way, think about the recipients of the blow—your children; they are the future generation that the adversary is after!

*Two people are better than one, for they can help
each other succeed. If one person falls, the other
can reach out and help. But someone who falls
alone is in real trouble.
Likewise, two people lying close together can keep
each other warm. But how can one be warm
alone? A person standing alone can be attacked
and defeated, but two can stand back-to-back and
conquer. Three are even better, for a triple-braided
cord is not easily broken.*

Ecclesiastes 4: 9-12 NLT

CHAPTER ONE

Living Single and Being Whole

1

Living Single and Being Whole

———— ⟨∽⟩ ————

I REMEMBER attending a leadership conference conducted by Dr Myles Munroe in 2003. The seminar was very informative. Dr Munroe is one of the most renowned motivational speakers I have had the opportunity of listening to. I don't attend seminars as much, but I went to this particular event and what was said inspired my life and added to the vision behind this book. During the session he spoke on relationships and the power of needs (the male and female needs). He mentioned something that was very profound in its meaning: he said, and I quote:

> 'The key to a good marriage is like an omelette
> that is only as good as the eggs. Whoever we yoke
> with determines the state of the marriage. It is
> more important to have the right male and female
> from the onset than to focus on the marriage.'

According to Dr Munroe's statement, divorce should not really be our problem if a marriage is as good as what the individual male and female are. Our singleness determines how good or how not so good the marriage will be.

God began the human race with a single person, not a couple. He created man first. And God said, 'Let us make man in our own image, after our own likeness.' (Genesis 1:26)

Hence the foundation of the human race did not start with marriage or a family, but a single whole individual – a male!

The first male and female were created single and whole, and we are from them so we ought to enjoy living as a single person before we join to another single, whole person. We must learn to be faithful as single people – the more we fill our lives with God's word, love and purpose, the more we can possibly determine the destiny of our marriage. Put it this way, it's like two single individuals, male and female, who have developed their lives and character, embraced the process of change in their lives, allowed God's love to fill their hearts and minds, and now wish to see God's will for their lives performed on earth. They are joined in marriage and the positive principles they have invested to develop positive character starts manifesting in their relationship. In other words what you sow when you are single is what you will reap in marriage.

Singles must concentrate on being whole in themselves, to know who they are, and to love who they are as beautiful creations before they can love another.

It is the unconditional love in us that extends to others. You must learn how to be faithful and responsible in your single life and individual walk with God – because when that which you have prayed and waited for is manifested in reality, it's because He has found you faithful and that you can handle and look after the increase. This also applies to 'married singles'. You want your spouse to show you that unconditional love, but what if they can't? You need to know God's love for yourself so that you can love your spouse and in return receive love back. Stop waiting for them to do it for you – take the step and know God's love for you. I know this is not easy when you have to deal with daily issues and circumstances in your life, but these are principles and I know that when you apply principles, however hard they may seem at first, they work in the end.

The greatest gift God ever gave us is His Son Jesus Christ – that was a gift of unconditional love; therefore we should accept the gift with open arms and learn how to grow in the image and likeness of His Son. As we do, we grow and develop in love for ourselves and love for others.

Paul[1] explains that single people have more time developing themselves and equally developing their relationship with God and their faith in Him. An unmarried woman can keep herself busy developing her spiritual relationship, but the same is not to be said for married people. Their interests are divided and as such can serve God best by looking after their responsibilities; a married woman should concentrate on her natural responsibilities and how to make her husband happy and that's okay because every marriage should be invested in – that's what pleases God. As a single woman, I had so much time on my hands. Apart from developing myself and my career, I was able to give my time to duties and ministries in the church. Paul explains that we should find the best way to serve God with no distractions. Single people have more time to discover who they are in Christ because there are no distractions from a mate. On the other hand, a married person can find out who they are in Christ through building their relationship with their mate.

This statement is so true in its meaning: single people have so much more time to spend in God's Presence discovering who they are.

When I was single, I was spending every moment I could get praying, reading and worshipping. Now that I am married, I spend time looking after my husband and daughters' needs and by the

---

1   *Scripture Reference 1 Corinthians 7:32-35*

time I am done, I'm too tired to spend time with God. All I want to do is get my rest ready for the next day. When I was single, I filled my prayer bank and now I go to that bank and get out my scriptures and my worship to God when I need it. This doesn't mean that I have stopped spending time with God. I have had to change the process of spending time with God when there are things to be done in my home. I implement this in my cleaning time and cooking time, and sometimes getting up an hour earlier to get my time with Him helps. It's important to me, as I need this to be effective in and for my family.

When singles concentrate on the Lord, they are nurturing their spirits with His Spirit through which they are being cleansed, set free from bondages, fears, anxieties, worries and doubts – all the baggages that could destroy a marriage if not dealt with. Embracing the single season means enjoying and developing oneself during singlehood to be complete in Christ, in order to be a complementary match for the right partner at the right time.

God's will is not for you to take your baggage of hurt and offload onto a partner; but to learn to offload your weight onto Christ. He conquered death and the issues you carry with you.

Embracing the single season is learning to let go of your old lifestyle and live in a renewed single lifestyle, preparing to be a proper mate to God's chosen partner for you. This means laying down your life for the other and praying for your mate in good and bad times regardless of the issues you face in the marriage.

In this renewed life, you are learning who you really are and God's desire for you. You are learning how to manifest God's potential for you to be successful in Christ and to be faithful and live righteously according to His principles.

To those who are married and didn't have the opportunity to embrace the single season of their own lives, I believe that you will learn how to do that in your marriage, not to the detriment of your marriage, but that your marriage relationship will live for God's purpose. I know of cases where people got married because they were burning 'sexually' and this is not to say they married the wrong person. I believe some married the right choice for them, but didn't learn how to live a fulfilled single life free from sorrows and issues of that life and as a result they are going through the process of discovering who they are in marriage. Who knows, maybe that was God's leading for them, for in it, they would develop in character.

Discipline is not an easy task to go through. Walking the narrow road is challenging but the truth of the matter is the older you are as a single, when you choose to live God's way, the more experience you will have to produce a successful marriage relationship. Be at the place in your single life where you can thank God for keeping you for His perfect will for marriage. Where you may be today may not make sense but it will when you meet your partner.

There is so much you can do to avail yourself to the Lord as a single person. The more effective you are as a single person is the extent to how effective you will be for your partner when you are married. Responsibility and accountability is the key. When you are responsible and accountable as single people then it is most likely that you will be responsible as a husband or wife, father or mother, pastor, evangelist or teacher and you will also know how to be accountable to your spouse.

The term divorce should not be used lightly. I have often heard single women discuss the issue of divorce lightly as if it is an alternative to consider if things in the relationship go wrong, in other words, hedging their bets should whatever they were looking for in a spouse is not what they get.

As a single woman you learn how to endure, be patient and understanding, how to give to another person and spend the rest of your life with that person making them and their life with you a happy one. God created the institution of marriage as a blessing.

Even though it brings a new level of progression with new issues to deal with, God never created marriage so that you can get divorced when you feel that you've had enough!

The Gospel of Matthew captured this.[2] The Pharisees tested Jesus by asking Him whether it was legal for a man to divorce a woman for any reason. Jesus explained that divorce wasn't an issue in the beginning because from the start of the creation, God made one man and one woman and as such a man's responsibility is to leave his maternal home and be united to his wife. They then are no longer two individual people, but one. And therefore if they are one united by God, no one has the right to divide them. To attempt to separate what He has joined together is instituting a divorce.

God didn't create marriage to end in divorce. In the beginning, He created one male and one female. When the right male finds the right female and makes her his wife he joins himself to her and nothing can separate them, not even divorce. No matter what issues they may encounter in their marriage, nothing can separate them.

When individuals learn to live a fulfilled single life, they will be ready to walk into a honourable institution of marriage. Even though marriage in itself can be challenging, the two who have become one will choose to walk the path because they are under no illusions as to what to expect no matter how challenging it may be.

There are some single people who out of the frustration have lost their focus in waiting and as a result have given up doing so. Presently, there are so many single seminars and conferences held to discuss the aspect of why there are so many mature singles. The

---

2   *Scripture Reference Matthew 19:3-6*

resolution seems to be to get on with life, enjoy yourself because it may never happen. There is nothing wrong in enjoying yourself, but it is important to enjoy it in the right way, discover who you are and what you possess and how it can be of benefit to others. If it is your destiny to be married, then why abandon the idea altogether?

There is such a thing as a purpose driven marriage, and when we understand what God meant when He created such a concept, then it will help those preparing to get married and those who are already married to build their relationship on His model. We will explore this topic in more detail in Chapter Seven, The Purpose Driven Marriage.

Promise me, O women of Jerusalem,
by the gazelles and wild dear, not to awaken love
until the time is right.

Songs of Solomon 2:7 NLT

Reflection Time

• How has being single enhanced your relationship with God?

• Reflect on your deliverance and the growth you've experienced through knowing and committing to your faith.

CHAPTER TWO

Evidence of Desire is Pursuit

2

Evidence of Desire is Pursuit

THE more fulfilled you are as a single person, the more accepting of the realities of marriage you become when you meet your companion. I have often heard women, myself included, express a sheer desire to be married. These conversations normally happen when women gather together over tea, pampering sessions, conferences and so forth. It's not the only topic discussed but it is by far the most popular. The main topic on the agenda, I'm sure you can guess is, 'Where are all the men?' or 'When will it be my turn?' Even if some refuse to admit it vocally, they think it.

To be honest, getting married or wanting to be married has nothing to do with the lack of men and or surplus of women available. Society and a routine lifestyle may have you believe that, but I don't believe that God intended there to be more men than women. I believe that for every woman or man who wants to be married, God fulfils that desire with a suitable match; and it takes an understanding of His purpose for marriage for that to happen. It can sometimes be challenging in marriage when you have an intimate relationship with God; but it can even be worse being with someone and not being so intimate with the God who created marriage. The same applies with the men. When they convene in group discussions the topic will almost certainly finds its way towards women, dating and marriage.

Such topics, even though interesting, can single out members in a group whose characteristics fit the topic and hence create a sense of unworthiness of having such a desire. Furthermore, it can also create stereotypes and false notions of how they want their spouse to be. It doesn't allow for one to be open minded or the flexibility to allow the Spirit of God to work in one's life.

It's common practice to focus your mind and efforts on things you would like to achieve, set goals to achieve your plans and go for it. The bible even says that the evidence of your desire is in your pursuit. If we apply this verse to daily practical living, how then do you actually go about pursuing a partner to marry without being a nuisance? Does the pursuit involve you investing the time in your personal appearance to look the part to catch the desired partner? Or scout singles' bars hoping you'll meet the man/woman of your dreams?

Perhaps, when you're out shopping, you hope that by chance you may bump into that nice young man or woman who happens to be buying dinner for one, reflecting their single status? All these ideas are good and I've seen how such tactics have worked for some people. Oh, and by the way, let us not forget speed and internet dating, which are other avenues to meet the man or woman of your choice. While these are acceptable to some and there have been testimonies of such unions, what about finding your mate through the old fashioned way – praying and seeking God for His best for you!

Reflecting on the statement, 'The evidence of your desire is in your pursuit', how do you pursue your desire in attracting God's best for you? From the past, there is one thing I know: you can try all the avenues to meeting that marriage partner of your choice (notice I said 'your choice') and in the end become so tired, frustrated and disappointed and settle for less. However, once you connect to the Principle Author of marriages, you will find that you are not spending time eliminating choices, but developing yourself to discover who you believe in your heart is right for you, and you them. God chooses the mate and through His process and His Spirit, He directs you to that person.

Having said this, there are couples who threw caution to the wind and went with their best judgement, and after 25, 30 or 40 years of marriage they are still together enjoying what they initially found in each other. These were not staunch Christians who professed the faith of religion, they didn't go to church 24/7 hoping that they would get married, they allowed life to happen to them and that was how they discovered each other.

I would like to say even though I had to wait on God, grow in my faith and get busy discovering my potential, it was through my faith moving with the Holy Spirit to be in the place for my husband to find me, and be a support to him, that it happened. This will not necessarily happen with every single individual looking for a life partner because every person has his or her own story and that is what makes the discovery unique. In the end, I had to let go of my own assumptions and inhibitions and allow time and patience and the process of maturity to grow in me, and that's how my own unique story happened.

What are you looking for in a suitable life partner? I know that we want all the perfect trimmings that come with a ready-made partner – but sometimes, we find it difficult to allow ourselves go through the process to be suitable for that partner and, let's face it, there is no perfect individual. A friend of my sister's once said in passing that, if she wanted to know who her husband was, all she had to do was submit her will, her time and her focus in prayer to God, but she didn't know if she was ready for God to reveal that to her yet. Dedicating the most part of your time in prayer, fasting and worship to receive direction from the Creator really means laying aside your own will and desires and most people are not ready for that because it really entails denying your flesh and feeding your spirit man. We live in a fast paced society where everything you want is available at the snap of a finger and the process in waiting to hear and get direction from God takes too long for some people.

I strongly believe God has a desired marriage partner for each and everyone of us, and he or she may be within an arm's reach away, but until we submit to His process, it may seem like the mate is hidden from us so that we can yield ourselves fully to His desired will for us and make ourselves available to Him through humility, patience, long suffering, endurance, and deliverance filled with His love. However, let's face it, not everyone will end up with their desired mate.

Marriage is meant to be a blessing; staying married years and years later takes the grace and mercy of God. Therefore, to enjoy His blessing is to realise that Jesus came to set us free from our old life. There are so many individuals who need to let go of attitudes that can keep them stagnant at a crossroad and these include pride, arrogance, haughtiness, vanity, and stubbornness. These are the characters that prevent us walking in and maintaining a healthy married relationship.

Most of us are unaware that we possess such characteristics that can scare suitable suitors away from wanting to spend the rest of their lives with us. Such attitudes that refuse to be acknowledged and dealt with by us can keep us outside of the blessings of being with a humble partner; and of course the flip side of that would be to take something that doesn't really belong to you because you believe your biological clock is ticking and that means being with a man who already has a family of his own.

We are in desperate times, these are the last days and we need to be sensitive to walking on the narrow road that God has chosen for us. Marriage is meant to be a blessing, a promotion, but also the ability to deal with greater responsibility because you have been trained during your single season.

There are so many women and men that I personally know of who are still being developed in their attitudes in their single season. This doesn't mean that they will be made perfect, but it means that some baggage needs to be removed from their minds in order to give yourself in matrimony to another. Their attitudes may not be apparent to some and others may not know how to shirk off such attitudes to move on. There are some individuals who believe that gathering all the material things in the world is enough to make them a suitable partner to a man or a woman. But it's not in the materials that you acquire that makes you a suitable partner but what is in you as a person, what you have identified as your talent and how it can be used to support a family and propel you into your destiny.

A very long time ago, a famous prophet in the bible named Isaiah prophesied that a time would come when women will be so desperate to be married that it wouldn't matter whether the man belongs to another woman, is not suitable for them or would not even look after them, just as long as they could remove the shame of being lonely and single.[1]

The reason for this is because there will be so few men left that women will be struggling to get married to remove the shame of being single. This is what is happening in the world at the moment. The only way a woman will marry her own husband is when she understands her essence and her purpose in Christ.

We can tackle this mindset by renewing our mind with the word of God, by understanding that Jesus Christ shed His blood at Calvary, that He took back the keys from hell for our freedom. It is only when you receive Him and realise the good news, that you will know you don't have to hide away in shame because you've reached a certain

---

1   *Scripture Reference Isaiah 4:1*

age and are still unmarried; you don't have to run after a man and appeal to him to marry you. You will know the true love of God, His protection and therefore you can believe in His Love for you to choose a man who has His (God's) heart to love you as you are.

A further explanation to the above verse can also mean that women are doing the matchmaking process themselves. They want to find a man, they want to convince him that they are a suitable match in a wife for him, they want to manipulate a man to marry them so that they can adopt his name. It almost seems as though women are struggling to produce results their way partly because they don't know God's way. Our life of independence has been a constant battle of struggle, strive and control.

Where is God's place in your life? He wants us to give up our struggles, our unconscious methods of manipulation to make things happen our way, and let Him have His way. Marriage is a blessing created by God, and He is the one who prepares us for it. However, before we walk into this level, the attitudes of struggle, striving and controlling has to be dealt with.

Isaiah said, after the Lord has washed away the (immoral) filth of the daughters of Zion (pride, vanity, haughtiness) and has purged the blood stains of Jerusalem from the midst of it by the Spirit and blast of judgement and by the Spirit and blast of burning and sifting, then the Lord will create over the whole site, over every dwelling place of Mount Zion and over her assemblies, a cloud and smoke by day and the shining of a flaming fire by night; for over all the glory shall be a canopy (a defence of divine love and protection).

> *And there shall be a pavilion for shade in the day-*
> *time from heat, and for a place of refuge and shelter*
> *from storm and from rain.* (Isaiah 4:4-6)

Ladies, let God's word renew your perception of how you see yourself and your environment; allow His Spirit to remove the filth stored in your heart and highlight the good qualities about you, to remove the coarse particles that hide you from your chosen partner seeing you. When He is satisfied that you are ready, then the Spirit of God will lead you to know and accept His chosen partner and you will not reject God's will nor will you question it because you understand your purpose and the essence of your life on earth.

Accepting God's choice for a mate shouldn't be a burdensome task to do. When you accept His leading, He promises to give you rest in the choosing; you can't know who is right for you when you're controlling the process. It's only when you let go of the burden, the anxiety of wanting to be hooked with a man for the sake of it, that you're likely to find what's right for you. Your Father wants to teach you through being humble and gentle in heart, and in doing so there is a peace that accompanies your choice and a clarity that clearly shows you that your own choice could in fact be wrong for you.[2]

Isn't it wonderful to know that we have a God who will do the match making for us. He will tell the brother who you are, and you don't have to do a thing except to be willing to take and receive God's blessing for you in a partner.

We are so used to doing things for ourselves that we don't know how to allow someone else to do things for us, especially if that someone's thoughts and ways are higher than ours. Our Maker is our Husband. He put in us the desire to be married, let Him bring the desire into reality in His own time.

> Before (Zion) travailed, she gave birth: before her pain came upon her, she was delivered of a male child.
> Who has heard of such a thing? Who has seen such things? Shall a land be born in one day? Or shall a nation be brought forth in a moment? For as soon as Zion was in labour, she brought forth her child.
> Shall I bring to the (moment of) birth and not cause to bring forth? Says the Lord. Shall I Who causes to bring forth shut the womb? says our God. (Isaiah 66: 7 -9 AMP)

---

2 *Scripture Reference Matthew 11:28-29*

God doesn't want His children to frustrate themselves into making things happen. Before Zion (Israel) travailed or felt pain, she delivered a child; a nation was conceived. He never intended us to give birth in pain. When we make things happen in our own human understanding or reasoning, we feel the pain, the struggle and frustration and we become tired and impatient, sometimes left with bitterness due to the struggle.

It's not our position as women to make things happen by forcing a man to spend the rest of their lives with us. God wants us to be married His way and not our way.

I remember a season where I was spending so much of my time in God's Presence – my worship found me fall in love with Him all over again. I went to bed worshipping Him and woke up with a light spring in my feet praising Him. It was an awesome time for me just being in His Presence.

One particular evening I was worshipping Him so intently – I heard the Spirit say to me from within, 'Ask and you shall receive.' I knew this was the Holy Spirit. Suddenly I could hear myself confirming the character of my soul mate as it was deposited in my heart. I saw the character of the man God had chosen for me; and I had the boldness to thank Him for my partner.

As I got up from where I was worshipping, I heard in my heart, 'And he will love you just the way you are.'

When you are wearing a new garment of righteousness, you are not trying to flaunt your best attributes to a man and hide the things you don't want him to see. This chosen man will love you just the way you are. You don't have to be perfect – just need to have a righteous heart to serve whoever God has chosen for you. You don't need 10 steps to getting and keeping a man; there is no secret to having a man run after you. A righteous heart will always allow God to bring His son to you at the appointed time.

> *He who finds a wife finds a good thing and obtains*
> *favour from the Lord.* (Proverbs 18:22)

Let the chosen man find you – don't go looking for him because you could be looking for trouble and you'll end up getting your heart broken. Your desire to be married should be pursued in the appropriate manner and that should be through Christ and in God.

As you pursue God, love Him, seek after Him, be obedient to what He calls you to do – get busy for Him, you are pursuing God's mate for you through Christ. I remember when I found Christ and made that commitment to serve Him. One night I lay on my bed ready to sleep and my question to Him came out – 'Lord what do I have to do to get married?' The following morning, a verse in the book of Psalms dropped straight into my heart.

> *Delight yourself also in the Lord, and He will give*
> *you the desires and secret petitions of your heart.*

This was a scripture I read a long time ago and my memory must have retained it because it came back to me when I needed it.

Another translation explains it this way: 'Do what the Lord wants and He will give you your heart's desire.'

The evidence of desire is in your pursuit – pursue God, pursue His ways and His instructions and He will bring to pass the desire to meet His choice for you.

As you take care of the spiritual and physical part of preparation, God will order your steps. It doesn't matter if you are attending a speed dating event, going shopping to buy dinner for one or even at a Christian fellowship party as long as you are in the right place and at the right time – that divine meeting can happen. Staying in Him is the key.

Hope deferred makes the heart go sick, but a dream (desire) fulfilled is a tree of life.

Proverbs 13:12

Reflection Time

- How do you know that your destiny is to be married?

- What evidence do you have that reflects your desire to be married?

- What steps or remedies do you have to prevent the desire to be married from overwhelming you?

CHAPTER THREE

Knowing Your Purpose

3

Knowing Your Purpose

Your Destiny Has Already Been Planned

I WOULD like to spend some time discussing the meaning of the word 'destiny'. Destiny is a powerful concept and it means the future that is certain to be for a person or thing. In other words, your destiny was already pre-planned for you to walk in it when you came into the world.

> *For we are God's masterpiece. He has created us anew in Christ Jesus, so we can do the good things He planned for us long ago.* (Ephesians 2:10 NLT)

Your name is part of your destiny; that is why it is important to have names that convey a positive message because every time your name is mentioned it reinforces what you will be in the future. I have heard names that don't reinforce a positive meaning, common names like Damian, which means to subdue. The dictionary meaning of subdue is to overcome and bring a person under control through force or persuasion. This conveys a negative meaning and is in direct opposition to an individual who is trying to discover his potential and move forward in the freedom and success to achieve. Every time you call the name Damian you are actually reinforcing the negative meaning to this person, which is to bring him under control through force.

The same way your parents pre-planned your name before you were born, is the same way God pre-planned a partner for you. This partner, whether you are a man or a woman, is part of your destiny and everything else concerning your life is in your destiny. Having said this, how do you handle a situation where you've discovered that the person you married is not really meant for you? Not part of your purpose?

I have met women and men who believe they married the wrong person and their choice took them down a spiralling slope of unhappiness in marriage. Some have taken it upon themselves to make the marriage work because divorce is not an option for them. Others who can't go on due to abuse, violence or other issues, have gone back to God for a way to deal with their demise.

And He will show them a way through the burden as He wouldn't want you to be overburdened where it will cause you to lose your peace. He knows what you're capable of handling.[1]

Sometimes this experience is an opening to discover your purpose and to help others from making choices that could destroy them.

Katherine Kuhlman's Mission
Katherine Kulhman was an example. Her destiny was to be an evangelist, and at the age of 16 she started her ministry assisting her sister and brother-in-law. She was soon on her own itinerating in Idaho, Utah, and Colorado, finally settling down in Denver in 1933 in the Kuhlman Revival Tabernacle. By

1 *Scripture Reference 1 Corinthians 10:13*

1935 she had built the 2,000-seat Denver Revival Tabernacle. She effectively used the media and established an influential radio ministry. Her marriage to an evangelist, who divorced his wife to marry Kuhlman, destroyed her Denver ministry. They continued to evangelise, but after about six years she left him and started over again on her own.

As in the case of Katherine Kuhlman, some choices can take you right off your course of destiny. But in realising your mistakes you can get right back on course, and use it as an opportunity to empower others.

Most single women and men are so involved in searching for a suitable partner to marry, we often keep the Holy Spirit out of the equation without realising it.

We believe that once we know what qualities we want, we simply need to start searching for it in the physical attributes such as looks, height, figure, bank balance, education and social background.

However God chooses differently. Perhaps in the physical world the attributes may be the initial requirements, but in God's Kingdom the principle is different and if we pray to Him to intervene, we have to allow Him to lead us His way.

There were so many instances were I thought God had revealed to me who my marriage partner was; now looking back I realise I was still choosing what I thought my physical eyes appreciated, thinking it was the Holy Spirit who put the desire for that person in my heart.

During this period, a particular verse in the bible caught my attention.[2] When Samuel was meant to choose a king for Israel, he was sent to Jesse's house. Jesse had seven sons and when Samuel saw Jesse's first son, Eliab, who was an extremely physically fit man, he naturally thought that Eliab would be a suitable king; but he was mistaken as

---

2 *Scripture Reference 1 Samuel 16:7*

he wasn't the chosen one. Most times we make the mistake of judging an outward appearance, but God can see the heart of a man and as such chooses from the heart and not the outward appearance.

I knew at that moment that I could no longer trust my own choice because I wasn't choosing God's purpose for me, I was choosing from my physical desire. You see people and their choices for us can disappoint us, but when we put our trust and hope in God, He will never let us down.

There is an increasing number of women and men who have altered the principles of God by choosing partners to have children with, instead of choosing a partner who is emotionally stable and strong enough to handle the ups and downs that marriage can often go through. Children and every other blessing should be an added benefit to such a union and not a reason to marry or be with someone.

We live in a world where the institution of marriage is no longer seen as sacred. Individuals are looking for some person to erase the loneliness and bring happiness to their spirit and soul and this is a very huge burden to put upon any individual. There are so many cases of single mothers who have children with a man who they had chosen through their physical desire, without really knowing what is in this man's heart. Can you trust him to stay with you, even when the going gets tough? Most of these women have been victims of men who were emotionally not ready to have a family. In the end, the man leaves the woman to deal with raising the child on her own, sometimes with no support at all.

Men have also suffered at the hands of a women who have abandoned their children to the man's mercy with no thought or care for the children.

Again this is down to making wrong choices and finally discovering that this relationship is no longer satisfying their needs. One thing I am certain of is that it is extremely difficult to stay the course when you are not walking in the chosen destiny you were created for.

I waited for my prayers for the right partner to be answered because I could not have courageously gone through marrying the wrong partner. I realised that I couldn't trust my own judgement as I had previously got it wrong so many times. Allowing God to have His way in me required a process of letting go to my own physical desires; letting go to what I thought was a suitable match for me because of my upbringing, and trusting my Destiny Maker to reveal in me His best partner for me.

There were times I wasn't walking according to the purpose I believe had been created for me, because I was looking for love in all the wrong places. I put this down to not understanding my potential and my role in life. The same applies to so many; we allow the hurts of past relationships to destroy our ability to discover who we are and the reason for our being.

I know of two individuals very close to me whose relationships could have destroyed their destinies. I will call them Friend A and Friend B.

Friend A

Friend A was visiting England for a while. It was on this holiday that she met her husband. He was a young man also looking to settle down and have a family. The only problem with this match was that unbeknownst to my friend, he already had a wife and child, which he had kept quiet about.

During the wedding preparations it came out that he was already married. The story he told was that the marriage wasn't real and it was arranged for immigration purposes. Even though she didn't feel like continuing, he some how managed to convince her that the marriage was only a marriage of convenience and divorce proceedings were already taking place. As so much preparation had already been done, including the meeting of both families, my friend decided to go ahead and marry this man after his divorce became final. Seven years later, with two children, her husband left her with a huge financial burden.

The man is now remarried with a child, resettled in another country and hasn't even signed the divorce papers. Friend A was able to pick up the pieces and today she has realised her gift, has two albums and travels to Africa as a missionary. Her close relationship with God made her aware of the lies her husband had told her about the first relationship and a child from the beginning that she didn't know about.

Friend B

Friend B met her husband through a friend. Although she wasn't attracted to him in the slightest, somehow when he proposed she found herself accepting his proposal. She was looking for someone to value her and she thought he would be the person. Little did she know that this man had an issue with infidelity and was under the control of his family. Even though he was married to her, he hadn't really left his paternal family, so her matrimonial home was always under the scrutiny of his mother, sisters and brothers. The man continued with his infidelity and the result was the birth of a child from one of his relationships.

After eight years of marriage, Friend B decided to move on as his continuous infidelity could put her at the risk of contracting a deadly sexual disease. She also wanted her children to grow up in a healthy, peaceful home. This decision brought her to a place where she had to struggle through hardship with her two children but, importantly, it also gave her freedom.

Today, her story has changed in the sense that her unfortunate relationship with her husband drew her close to God, which enabled her achieve a masters degree. She has relocated to another country and works as an ambassador for human rights.

These two women are an inspiration to me; having been through their mishaps, they sought the truth, took courage and with boldness allowed the truth set them free from such unfortunate circumstances to move into purpose.

Sometimes you have to be wrong to be right and in both circumstances, these ladies made wrong choices, but it led them on to the right path.

The men they chose had issues of their own that were not resolved before they took the next step and it eventually ended up with others being hurt by this – hurting people hurt other people. Both women had doubts at one stage not to go through with the marriage, however their lack of understanding about their destinies and who they are meant they were left to continue walking up the aisle.

Some of you may have decided to move in with a partner and discover whom you're living with before the next step called marriage is discussed. This may have serious consequences for others, such as children and the people involved if it doesn't end in marriage.

My friends eventually found their way back, but what about those who stay on the wrong path for not understanding where they fit in? Those who stay in situations in the hope that one day the partner will change, or because they cannot see themselves being alone and making changes that will benefit them and their future?

It doesn't matter how ready a man or a woman is to move to the next level and marry, if they're not fully prepared before taking that step, it ends up leaving them and so many others a casualty.

While it is important to note that there is someone for everyone, it's also crucial to realise that there is a right man for a woman and vice versa. We just need to allow God to prepare us for them.

Our purpose is already prepared and our marriage partners are in that purpose. Our responsibility, therefore, is to first discover who we are in Christ and where we're meant to operate from. You'll then find that everything else needed is in that location.

A Wife for Isaac: The Story of Abraham, Isaac, Rebekah and Eliazar

This story depicts how a father who so loved his son wanted him to marry a woman who would support him and be a companion to him through the good and bad times.[3] Abraham was getting old and would soon pass on, so this was his way of ensuring that his son continued to follow in his footsteps and bring to manifestation the Promise told to Abraham by God. The story holds a principle that we can all be encouraged to learn and live by.

Abraham instructed his oldest serving servant, Eliazar, to go in search of a woman with certain credentials, and the servant found Rebekah. In the same way, God wants His sons to marry good wives so He sends His Spirit in search of such women; a woman who has already been prepared by God's Hand, an 'in the beginning woman'.

> *Houses and riches are the inheritance of fathers;*
> *and a prudent wife is from the Lord.* (Proverbs 19:14)

Abraham calls his oldest servant to go and choose a wife for his son Isaac. He gives him clear instructions of what to look for in a wife for Isaac and this includes not choosing a woman from the Canaanite tribe where Abraham had settled; rather he wanted Eliazar to go back to Abraham's country and choose a wife from amongst his relatives*.

Isaac had no idea that his father was planning to find a wife for him. This agreement was only kept between Abraham and his servant.

---

3   *Scripture Reference Genesis 24: 2-4*

God is very interested in the man He has chosen for His daughters. It goes beyond our own will and the will of the man. Just as Abraham instructed his servant, God through His Spirit finds a wife for His sons. The men may say that they want to be married, however the list of features they want in a woman doesn't sometimes line up with God's list and therefore God takes it upon Himself to search for a wife with the qualities of a helpmate who will develop in her husband the ability to be the man God has predestined him to be.

At the same time, He is also working in the man a desire to look for a woman, someone who will help him to get to his destiny and in the process build his wife into the woman she is called to be. This is why it is important for women to yield to the Spirit of God and draw closer to Him.

Abraham took the task of choosing a wife for Isaac away from his son (although this does not happen much in the present day). His purpose was already chosen before he was born and Abraham was going to see to it that he followed God's plan for his son's life. Abraham's instruction to the servant was specific; he was to find Isaac a wife of the same faith.

A man learns to submit to God so that he can humbly receive and accept the help that the woman he marries offers him. Most times it is not easy for a man to submit to God and that is where the wife's support can help her husband. Not by telling him, but by praying to God.

A reflective question ladies should ask themselves is what kind of husband would they like to marry? Be honest and truthful to yourself. Write down these qualities on a piece of paper. When you have finished, look at these qualities and ask yourself if you have the qualities within you to be a wife to the man you want to marry. If you believe that you need to mature in some parts of your character, ask the Holy Sprit for His help and be prepared to yield to His training in that area so that you will be ready for the man when he comes your way.

The same applies to men: write a list of characteristics and positive attitudes you are looking for in a woman. When finished, ask yourself if you have the qualities ready to be a husband to such a woman. If not, ask the Holy Spirit for His help to prepare you for such a woman, so that you don't miss her when she crosses your path.

Abraham further instructed his servant that the woman he chooses had to be willing to follow him back to Canaan. This woman had to be confident in her convictions to follow her desire. If she was not willing, then she wouldn't be the wife for Isaac.

> *And if the woman should not be willing to go*
> *along after you, then you will be clear from this*
> *oath; only you must not take my son back there.'*
> (Genesis 24: 8 AMP)

A willing character is a necessary quality to have in a woman. This character goes a long way; we have to be willing to follow the Holy Spirit to wherever our destiny takes us. In most cases it means stepping out from the place where we are too comfortable to make some positive changes.

As we develop our relationship with God, He helps us let go of the things that prevent us from moving further to accomplish new ground in our lives for Him. We are delivered from our fears, the idols that we don't realise that we worship, to stand alone trusting in Him, ready to move at His instruction.

It is through the renewing of our mind daily that we can know God's perfect will for our lives.

Knowing your purpose (God's Perfect Will) entails you thinking differently, renewing your mind set. Perhaps there was a particular way you did things, and it could've been working for you until you've come to a certain point in your life and you find that you're not getting the results you were used to getting. God's perfect will for your life, which also entails His perfect partner for you, comes with a transformed mind set, a new way of thinking, a changed outlook to life. You can't see your partner until your outlook on life changes.[4]

Eliazar Discovers Rebekah

When Eliazar left Abraham, he set off to a town where his master's brother Nahor had settled. There, he made his camels kneel beside a well outside the town. It was evening and the women were coming out to draw water from the well.

As he prayed, he made a request that if he asked one of the women to give him a drink from their jug, and she agreed and went further to give his camel water to drink too, then he would take this as a sign that this woman was chosen as a wife for Isaac.

Before he had finished praying he saw a young woman named Rebekah coming towards him with her water jug on her shoulder. She was beautiful and old enough to be married. As she went to the spring and began filling her jug with water, Eliazar the servant ran to her and begged her for water to drink from her jug.

She obliged the servant and gave him water to drink from her jug and when he had finished she also offered to give his camels water to drink until they had enough. Eliazar watched her in silence wondering whether this was the chosen lady for his master's son. Finally when the camels had finished drinking, Eliazar took out a gold ring for Rebekah and two large bracelets for her wrists – a gift for her kindness to them.

---

4 *Scripture Reference Romans 12:2*

In questioning Rebekah, Eliazar discovered that she was in fact a distant relation to Abraham's brother Nahor and they had room for Eliazar to stay that night. When the servant met Rebekah's brother Laban, he was eager to tell him the reason he was visiting and everything Abraham had asked him to do. Eliazar explained that he was to go to his master's country to find a wife for Isaac and furthermore, this woman should be willing to follow him back to Isaac; any woman who refused this was not meant to be Isaac's wife. Abraham wanted a woman who shared the same faith as his son Isaac so it was crucial that Eliazar had to go back to Abraham's country – Canaan.

Rebekah's family had accepted Eliazar and knew that God sent him.[5] They agreed for Rebekah to follow Eliazar back to Isaac. However, they were not prepared for the immediate change that was about to happen in Rebekah's life; they wanted more time with her. They wanted Rebekah to stay with them for at least 10 more days before she left for her new life.

The servant wasn't prepared to consider this as he was operating under the instructions of Abraham. There wasn't any more time to be wasted and he didn't want to hinder his fortune in finding Rebekah.

When you are operating in purpose, you're aware of the time, your season and what needs to be done to prepare for this. People in purpose are not concerned about the barriers; they must find a way forward.

Eliazar couldn't afford 10 more days with Rebekah's family.

Her family meant well, but they would have cost Rebekah her destiny had she agreed to stay longer with them. The servant was following Abraham's instructions and Rebekah, who understood that she was about to take part in setting in motion her

---

5 *Scripture Reference Genesis 24:55-56*

own destiny, knew she had to seize the opportunity the moment it was presented to her. This was her time, her door of purpose had been opened to her. She had to walk straight through. As a result, when her family asked for her decision in the matter, she chose to follow the servant immediately.

My transition from single to marriage wasn't an easy one where others were concerned. I have also heard this from others who had to make choices to move in their purpose. Most times when two people meet, it would make sense that they get to know each other first, to understand character and attitudes before they say 'I do'. It wasn't like that in my situation.

Of course we were mature and knew what was right for us, but our families kept on putting restraints on us as if we didn't know what we were doing. Their fears made it look like we were making decisions that didn't make sense to their understanding.

Look at the story of Mary the mother of Jesus, when Angel Gabriel appeared to her to announce the birth of Christ. His first words to her were: 'Hail, O favoured one [endued with grace]! The Lord is with you! Blessed (favoured of God) are you before all other women.'

Mary's destiny was to bring forth the Messiah into the world. She was a virgin engaged to marry Joseph a Carpenter. The appearance of the angel was to inform Mary that she had been chosen amongst other woman to bring a vision into the world. Imagine what it would have done to her reputation? A virgin, not yet married, who was pregnant – what a shame! No one would understand the vision Mary had to carry. Think about the taunts, rebukes and rejection she would have had to face because she had the grace to carry this vision. It didn't matter what she would have been subjected to because she had a grace that enabled her to carry something that didn't make sense to outsiders looking in. This is the same grace that I had.

We didn't court for very long. We knew it was the will of God and, furthermore, we were setting our destinies in motion to move forward in spite of those around us who said it wasn't a good idea because we had only dated for a short time, which wasn't enough to know who we would be spending the rest of our lives with. They made clear their fears, but we were moving in faith because we had that grace upon us to see to it that God's vision for us was birthed in the appropriate timing.

Furthermore, the grace available to us to carry this vision through was open for a limited time and our role was to ensure that we were walking in line with God's Spirit, and not that of man's.

Those round us couldn't see it because it wasn't their destiny, so they couldn't handle it the way we could.

Rebekah also took that bold step when she said she would follow Eliazar to a country she had never been before, talk less of a man she didn't even know existed.

Women who have given God the decision to choose a partner for them should follow in Rebekah's footsteps and be willing to move, even when it may not make sense to our own human understanding.

If you've given God the decision to choose a partner for you, then follow in Rebekah's footsteps and be willing to move when it is time, even when it may not make sense to your own human understanding. Sometimes, family, out of concern, may be doing harm because they do not always see God's preparation for us. I am simply saying understand where they are coming from but do not ignore God's plans for your life. By walking with God, He will always give you favour with your family. Sometimes, choosing purpose may bring disapproval to those close to us – it is God who gives us the grace and strength to take up His call and follow Him despite the disapprovals from others. His will is always greater than the will of our family and friends – as long as we are not intentionally harming any one.

I want to take a moment to discuss Rebekah's qualities and why I think she was chosen for Isaac.

The Qualities of a Potentially Good Wife

I have seen couples that to the naked eye may not suit each other, but in the eyes of God, are a match made in heaven. If we want to be cruel in our thoughts, we may think, what does this man see in this woman? Or what does this woman see in this man? When two people come together, they see qualities in each other that would support, empower and propel them to build a godly nation and raise godly children, not to talk of achieving certain goals ordained by God for the destiny of the relationship.

Rebekah was a notable lady whose qualities caught the eye of Abraham's servant well enough for her to be given a gold ring and two bracelets within minutes of meeting him. There are qualities in us that will attract us to the kind of person we are looking for. It can be described as a perfume that catches the smell of a hunter looking for a particular kind of prey.

Rebekah had qualities that were very unique to Eliazar, as he knew what he was looking for and could identify it when he saw it. Such qualities were:

WILLINGNESS – Rebekah quickly lowered her jug from her shoulder to give Eliazar a drink. When he had finished drinking, she immediately drew water for his camels until they had had enough to drink. A wife is not necessarily perfect; rather willing and eager to assist.

HOSPITABLE – Her gift was to provide help and hospitality. She was prepared to render her gift to Eliazar and his camels until they where fully satisfied.

FOCUSED – Rebekah knew that Eliazar's presence had something to do with her purpose and she wasn't going to let it pass her by, that is why she agreed to follow him back to Canaan.

DILIGENCE – She carried out the task of helping Eliazar with care and perseverance.

HUMILITY – Rebekah seemed to have come from a wealthy background. She informed Eliazar that her family had plenty of room for him to spend the night and enough food to feed his camels. Nevertheless, this didn't stop her from rendering a service to someone she had never met before in spite of her comfortable background. Humility is a beautiful quality to have.

PRUDENCE – Rebekah was sensible and careful in answering Eliazar's questions about her family, because she had exercised good judgement to help him. She knew that his gift of the gold ring and bracelets was an indication that he wanted to know more about her.

RESOURCEFULNESS – In my opinion this is a major. A woman has to be resourceful, must know how to make things happen, create funds, wealth and so forth. When you marry and start having children or more children, the last thing you want is to build your professional career at the expense of their development, that is why it's important to create opportunities, avenues where you don't lose out on making money even though you're not in a conventional job. Nowadays women are creating their own jobs and what better way to do this around your home. Set up your office in your home. It gives your children a sense of security to know that you are around. Being a mother doesn't mean you stop earning, it just means you change the way you earn.

Furthermore, a man respects a woman who has built something of her own, a legacy to leave behind for her own children and children's children. This is not for you to lord it over the man, but to instil in you a sense of confidence in God who has done great things for you by making you resourceful. This is a quality in a woman that every household should have.

Women have such qualities and more. We hide them because we don't want to be taken advantage of so we portray a hard exterior which often times frightens a prospective partner away.

I can understand what women face in a hard-edged society. Struggling on their own to make ends meet can hide away the soft, meek and mild individual that you are and replace it with a tough, hardened person that you're not. We hide ourselves behind the façade and expect someone to love us and most times it's not as easy to meet such a person. Waiting for a partner alone is enough to chip off that hardened exterior and present us in an attractive humbling way to a man or woman who wants to be there for us. You will see your desires manifest in your own lives as you continue to walk in a willing (open) and obedient heart.

I strongly believe that while we wait on God for a suitable marriage partner and we are focused on Him, no one will delay our blessing, because at the right time the promise will surely manifest. Why? Simply because you are in relationship with the Giver of the blessing and you will know when it is time to take the next step and no one, not even you, can stop it.

Rebekah was in a relationship with God, and that was why she was able to discern her moment of opportunity. There is no point looking for a man to marry when God has taken care of it for you. Some women develop a role in church because they are looking for a husband; magazine articles advise women to become more active in their communities, local churches and other social spots to meet a husband. There are also etiquette classes in America teaching women how to catch a wealthy husband. There is so much misinformation in our society today that women don't know who they are or where they are going.

I once spoke to a gentleman who mentioned that his experiences of women have fallen into two categories; they are either desperate or uptight. For a man to say such a statement illustrates the kind of women that he has surrounded himself with; notwithstanding there are still a lot of genuine, beautiful, wise women who are looking for a suitable man to produce a family and make a home with.

However, the truth of the matter comes back to developing that intimate God relationship. When we love Him, read and act on His Word, the Holy Spirit will lead us slowly into the right location.

During a singles prayer meeting an anointed woman spoke by the inspiration of the Holy Spirit and told me that I have a burning desire to be married, because He has made me to be a home-maker. She explained that this desire was not from my personal desire and I need not be ashamed of it, because it is God who has given me this desire. This burning desire to be married directed me to pursue it God's way, by embracing my faith with my whole heart, enjoying the process of developing my relationship with God as though all that mattered was Him and joyfully serving Him regardless of whether I was married or not.[6]

A close friend decided to take matters into her own hands. She was tired of waiting and decided to get help via internet dating. She signed up to a Christian website dating agency and was introduced to a number of bachelors in other countries. One bachelor in particular based in Canada continued writing and subsequently expressed an interest in her. She committed herself by supporting him in making a trip to meet with her on two occasions. This gentleman disappointed her by not keeping his appointment with her even though he had financial support from her. On the first occasion he claimed he had a major accident where his car was badly damaged and as a result couldn't keep the appointment.

6   *Scripture Reference Psalm 37:4 AMP*

On the second occasion, he claimed that he had come as far as Heathrow Airport and misplaced his phone where her number and other information was stored, he slept in the airport because he had no way of supporting himself and took the next flight back to Canada the following day. What a likely story this was. My friend was disappointed as she spent time and money and her emotions.

A year later I asked her if she ever discovered what happened to this man from Canada and she said that she took matters into her own hands by searching and, as such, trouble found its way to her doorstep. There is an old proverb which states, 'he who finds a wife, finds a good thing, and obtains favour …'

My friend had taken matters into her own hands by finding a husband, when it should have been the other way round. Men are natural hunters and they enjoy hunting for their helper.

I'm not saying internet dating is wrong. This was her experience and her conclusion. I believe the Holy Spirit can lead us to the right place. When you concentrate on your purpose in the right way and you get on with your business with the right intentions, what you're praying for will find its way to you. It takes patience and time to develop the right character; and when God is satisfied with His work in you and in your partner, then He brings you both together to start a life of building. The blessings of the Lord makes rich and adds no sorrow to it; your singlehood season is molding you to handle the next phase of life in marriage that it brings.

A man who decides to take a wife must know who God is to him. It also means that he is prepared to protect, cultivate, be responsible and humble to receive the wisdom of help deposited in the woman to help them accomplish their vision.

I believe that most men have to deal with fear to move to the next phase in their lives, especially when it comes to marriage.

Taking on the responsibility of having someone else being accountable to him, having to lead another individual who will be dependent on him, means he must also step up in his ability to provide and protect a family. This can become a burden as they start to wonder if such a move is the right move. As time goes on, if not careful, they start to rely on their own capabilities in leading their wife simply because they don't want to fail in such a task. To others it may come across as an arrogant attitude – they know it all; they don't need help, especially from a woman. They've got the car, the house, a career; all they need to make it complete is a beautiful woman on their arm to make them look good; this is a symptom of fear. But when you meet a man who has died to his natural desires and wants, he would be looking for a woman who has godly wisdom in her, a woman of knowledge and prudence – a woman who is yielding to God's work in her so that she is able to help her man.

That is what a man needs and when she is ready, he will recognise her to be the bone of his bone and the flesh of his flesh – he will spiritually see his wife, which goes beyond the natural.

This should be the testimony of a man who has allowed challenges in life to humble him. I know that physical attributes should not be left out of the equation, but choosing a wife should not be dependent on this.

Pride kills our desires, our dreams, hopes and our spiritual sight. Once God is satisfied with the man's character, he will have his own vision; he will be able to receive God's wisdom from his wife and will lead you according to God's instructions. Above all, he will love you just the way you are. That is God's intended partner for you.

When Abraham organised that his servant go and find a wife for Isaac, he wanted a chosen woman who was going to help his son fulfil the promise and purpose of his life. In the same manner, a man chooses a woman who will help him fulfil his purpose. Therefore, every woman is prepared as a necessary resource for her husband to achieve his vision. That in itself is the evidence of a destiny already chosen for you before you have even started. Isn't that wonderful!

Making the Right Choice

It's not always easy making the right choices where matters of the heart are concerned, especially in choosing a marriage partner.

The traditional talk is that a man chooses a woman to marry; and as such, a woman should be honoured that she has been chosen. There is an element of this statement that is true, but I also believe that a wise woman is also responsible for accepting the choice of a man who has chosen her. Her wisdom is able to direct her to believing that such a man is able to build, protect and provide for her.

So, even though a man chooses, the ultimate decision is left with the woman to accept the man's choice.

I am a great believer that operating in purpose will lead you to the partner that is right for you. Rebekah's location at the well positioned her in purpose where Eliazar saw her and her ultimate move to follow the servant to her husband Isaac ensued.

Your purpose supports you to make choices in line with your life and that also includes the partner suitable for you. It's more like the purpose is your direction and anything that will take you out of your purpose is not a choice to even consider.

In March 2002, I had a very vivid dream that gave me an idea about the kind of partner that would build me further in my purpose as I would him. I didn't understand the dream, but a year later as I was narrating the dream from my journal to my sister I found myself understanding God's intentions for me.

The dreams depicted weddings. In the first wedding, I was marrying a man I knew. In the dream, I wasn't the exuberant bride; in fact I wasn't happy that I was marrying this person. The ceremony was a very quiet one with no fuss. At that moment I woke up and realised it was a dream and happily went back to sleep.

In the second dream, this wedding was the opposite of the first dream. In this dream, I was marrying another person that I didn't know. This wedding was a big ceremony; everyone seemed to be involved in organising the ceremony. I was happy I was marrying this person; there was an internal joy and peace. In the dream I overheard a woman discussing with another lady her displeasure in the fact that I was marrying the man that she had wanted for herself.

My heart went out to her and I found myself interrupting the conversation. I didn't have any anger, only the compassion to reach out to her and encourage her to move closer in her faith and believe that her own husband will find her soon. I promised to contact her on my return from my honeymoon and I woke up.

Nine years after the dream, now married, I have been able to understand what both dreams and wedding ceremonies meant. The first wedding wasn't a big affair and even though I was marrying someone I already knew, I wasn't happy.

The second wedding was a big affair and the opportunity for me to operate in my purpose—to reach out and empower women. The second wedding was the platform for me to develop in my purpose, it offered fulfilment and the joy of life; a life where I would continue to develop in my relationship with God and His call for me. This man who God had for me would not be a barrier to my purpose, he would build me in my purpose. It wasn't about the physical ceremony even though that was important; it was more that the wedding was a fulfilment to God's promise of marriage for me. The first wedding was single, no vision. The second wedding was a marriage offering me abundance and life fulfilment.

Today, I can happily say that the man I am married to falls in line with the second dream and my marriage is a platform for both of us to walk in purpose. My husband has never posed as a barrier for me to develop in my purpose and as such I am able to be a wife without limitations and a mother to my children. I have a joy in doing it because I have been allowed to fulfil my purpose.

On hindsight, it really wasn't about the wedding, but being fulfilled in what I am called to do through the person I am called to build with. Both dreams were a direction showing me which one would offer me the desire of my heart; all I had to do was choose.

You can make many plans, but the Lord's purpose will prevail.

Proverbs 19:21

Reflection Time

• What do you believe is your PURPOSE?

• What are your GIFTS?

• How are you using your gifts to fulfil your purpose?

CHAPTER FOUR

A Woman's Power is in Submitting God's Way

4

A Woman's Power is in Submitting God's Way

In 2002, I had a dream that explained to me how a woman's most powerful tool is submission. In this dream, I was having a driving test and was trying to park my car in a bay parking area. It seemed so simple, but for some reason, after several attempts, I couldn't get it to align within the required area. Those who were waiting for me started getting restless and, just as they were about to give up on me ever trying to park the car, I eventually succeeded.

In reflecting on the dream, what spoke loud and clear to me was that it took me several attempts to do something that looked very easy to do at a first attempt. Suddenly a light came on in my mind; I was never called to be in the driving seat of my marriage. The anointing to lead in marriage has been given to my husband because he is the head and not I. Sometimes, women decide to take up a calling that was never given to them and when they do this, they become frustrated and insult their husbands because they are not doing what they feel their husbands should be doing. That was why what really looked simple for me to do was really difficult.

God has anointed His sons with the ability to lead; lead through His Grace. We are partners in marriage, but we also have specific roles that we operate in. In God's Kingdom it is not up to us to reassign the roles that go against His order.

We should accept our roles and be happy to serve our husbands in their roles as leaders in the family. It is true that God anoints women with wisdom; but it is the wisdom to help our husbands into their positions and not lord it over them. In the same way, He anoints his sons to receive and lead. Before we discuss the roles we play in marriage, I would like to look into the wisdom and knowledge women should be walking in before getting married. To illustrate this, I would like to direct you back to our main scripture text in Genesis.

When Rebekah discovered that Isaac was the man she travelled all that way for, she took her veil (a piece of transparent material worn over the face for concealment, it can also be used to enhance an appearance) and covered herself with it[1].

This act symbolised her submission to Isaac.

I have often met Christian women who through prayer have had a revelation of their partner's identity. I certainly don't dispute that this is possible, after all anything is possible with God, especially when you're in relationship with Him. However, it's important to understand what spirit may be operating; there is deception operating in the Christian community and having dreams that a man may be your husband can be deceptive.

Having said this, there are people who have had a revelation of their partner in dreams. My advice is that such a spirit should be tested against God's Word. This has also happened to me, and I can look back in hindsight and see that I was being deceived by

---

1   *Scripture Reference Genesis 24: 64-65*

my own desires to be married.

Even if you believe that you discern that a particular person may be your marriage partner, wait for God's Word, reveal it to the person and if it's the man he will approach you as confirmation about what you believe.

I didn't end up with this person, but the lesson I learnt from this relationship was accomplished in the sense that I understood what being a helpmate was all about and a large majority of it was to pray for his footsteps to be directed onto the right path to his purpose. Maybe God used him and that season of my life to teach me one of the roles of a helpmate.

The whole experience taught me how to be patient, believing that my desire would come to pass in the fullness of time. In the meantime what should I be doing whilst I am waiting? Continue with life, adhering to my Christian principles and discovering my reason for being—purpose.

God doesn't need help from us to do His work. All He requires is for us to stand and believe that what He revealed, if true, will surely come true in the fullness of time.

It is our responsibility to cover ourselves with the spiritual garment of righteousness, protect our hearts so that we do not become frustrated and angry, directing such feelings towards the man, when it has nothing to do with him and everything to do with God.

My marriage has seen me apply what I learnt during that period of my life. So the experience I had with this young man wasn't a waste of time.

Rebekah Submits to the Promise

Rebekah's character is unlike many of the women in today's society. She was pure hearted, hospitable, eager to please and was a joy to her family. Such qualities wouldn't have problems in submission. Her innocence allowed her to follow a stranger.

The modern woman needs a bout of Rebekah's innocence. Not every man who may not have the means is looking to take from you; maybe he needs the resources you have to build him into his role. Our hard exterior and in depth experience coupled with maturity makes us suspicious of the man who may not be as established as you are. This does not mean he is not God's chosen for you; you will need to see him through the eyes of Christ to see God's best for you in him. And, if he is chosen by God, what a wonderful destiny he has.

When Rebekah saw Isaac and asked the servant who this man was, the servant told her that Isaac was the man she would spend the rest of her life with. She immediately took her veil and covered her face, which symbolised submission to Isaac. He was her covering so she accepted the covering in Isaac. She accepted her destiny willingly, with no questions asked. It is acceptable to say that Rebekah submitted to the Call. That promise was God-given so she was actually submitting to God so that He could use her in Isaac's life.

Women are very emotional beings. We also have a strong nurturing side to our person that can sometimes prove to be a detriment rather than a positive. If we are yoked to the wrong mate, we are submitting in the wrong way. The tendency would be for the man to use it against us. Submission is an act of love, but with the wrong person it could be an act of slavery (door mat) and not servant hood. When it's the former, a woman could lose her identity, her self esteem, her wholeness because she is trying to make her mate happy and yet nothing she can ever do will make him happy so he starts to use it against her by pulling her down with him. Not understanding her destiny and understanding who she is will eventually see her living in her shadow because she isn't maximising her potential and he is not cultivating her.

I have coached and mentored women who know their purpose and want to start running in it, but sadly are not going anywhere because there is a weight they're carrying. This weight looks like a partner who doesn't know his role in her life. Sadly the woman is at a loss as to what to do.

She has to make the choice between staying with this partner for fear of being alone for the rest of her life or concentrate in building her purpose and risk the loss of a relationship. I narrate the story of The Pearls to help them make choices in line with their purpose.

The Real Pearls
A father has the responsibility of reading a bedtime story to his daughter every night. On one occasion after the story, he asks his daughter to hand him some pearls she hangs onto as if she is protecting them from whoever will take them away from her. She cries and says, 'No Daddy, I can't give these to you, I just can't.' Her dad doesn't push it any further and decides to try again another time.

The second night after reading another bedtime story, he asks her again for the pearls she is holding. Again she refuses, saying how she won't have anything else like it and wants to keep them.

The third night instead of reading a bedtime story, he decides to ask for the pearls straight up. This time she looks at the pearls, looks at her dad, looks at the pearls and as she glances back at him with a sombre face, she reluctantly hands her father the pearls. Immediately, her father reaches into his pocket and hands her a beautifully gift wrapped jewellery box, she opens it and finds these beautiful pearls very similar to the one she handed her father. The difference was that the ones her father gave her were the real pearls and the pearls she reluctantly handed her dad were the fake ones.

How does this story apply practically? Some women are holding onto illusions of a relationship with men who are not prepared to cultivate them or build them in their purpose once married. At the moment the relationship looks like he's all for you, purpose and potential, but once married, your life becomes a reality of hell.

The real marriage partner is on your pathway of purpose.

As you're discovering your purpose and operating in it, he will come through that avenue, that's why it's important to discover your purpose. You have to let go of the man you're holding onto to, so that the man who is really for you can make his way into your life. If you continue to hold onto a man who doesn't belong in your purpose and destiny, you will find that everything, even your purpose, will begin to be at a stagnant place until you let him go.

Some women are submitting to the wrong man in the wrong way. You don't submit to a man who hasn't made you his wife. You are giving him authority over you without him paying the price. Such emotional trauma can be avoided. I know it can be hard to let go of someone you've become complacent with; but it's even harder living the rest of your life with someone who is not right for you and may never accommodate your growth. When you let him go and everything else that he stands for that doesn't belong in your destiny, you won't be supported by crutches, but by God who promises to uphold you with the Right Hand of His Righteousness.

Any man ready to marry you God's way should also be submitted to God too. When you submit to a man who is submitted to God, it doesn't matter his lack of material resources, he will always receive wisdom from you, even if it doesn't seem like it at the time. He will go away and give it some thought and allow the Holy Spirit speak to his spirit to receive direction. Don't forget this man is meant to be leading you and protecting you; isn't it fair that he knows God for himself?

If You Love Someone—Set Them Free!

There was a time in my life I had hopes to marry a man that I thought ticked all the right boxes. He to be well educated, went to the right schools, had a good career, was socially connected and furthermore enjoyed playing rugby (a sport that only a certain type of man would play). I was dating him for close to five years and nothing was happening. No progress, only dating. As I tried to bring the 'where are we going' conversation, he would stop me by replying 'I have nothing to give you'. I didn't understand what he meant and I would find myself asking my men friends and girlfriends what such a response meant.

I suppose they were trying to explain it in simplest terms, but my failure to want to understand what he meant was blocking me from understanding what others were trying to explain to me about what he meant.

One evening, on my way home from a publishers' meeting, I was hit by a car while crossing the road. I wasn't in the slightest bit injured, though I had time off to recover from shock, but the days that preceded the accident caught my attention. I started singing a well-known Sting (formerly from the group Police) song... 'If you love somebody, set them free... free, free, set them free...'

I couldn't make out why I was singing this song in my head, but it later dawned on me that this was a message to me. If I love someone I need to set them free. What Sting doesn't add in his lyrics is that if you set them free and they come back they were yours to begin with; but if they don't come back then they were never yours in the first place.

And that was my test. If I say I really love this guy and what I want and believe I am worth doesn't seem to be happening, I need to set him free. I don't have any right to make him do what he is not willing and really ready to do. I had to set him free not knowing whether he would come back to me.

It was a very hard thing to do, but nevertheless, I obeyed the message from within. Once I did it, so many other things in my life started to move in a positive direction. It's as if being with him was holding up my destiny; but the minute I let him go, things started happening.

Eventually my destiny led me to travel to another country to promote my book and introduce my Life Coaching profession. It was on this travel that I met my husband, and it wasn't even a struggle. He saw me, pursued me and made his intentions towards me very clear.

It took me letting go of something that I thought was real but wasn't, to get something that was very real, and it was when I was busy doing what I was passionate about. To express my feelings, I wasn't desperate for marriage. I was quite happy to live the rest of my life writing and travelling and furthermore believing that if I was to be married, it didn't matter if I was on the remotest of islands, God knew who would be right for me and in due time I would meet him.

I didn't need to help my husband to find me; he just found me and knew who I was. I was the one that needed confirmation, because I didn't want to go through another five years waiting on someone who may not be right for me and me for him.

I have met women who have said that they couldn't help the suspense any longer: they needed to inform this man that he is their husband. We inform them what we believe God has told us, instead of praying that God should speak to the man to show them who you are to him. When you start helping God out, it makes you as a woman look ugly, desperate, controlling, frustrated—qualities that men run ten thousand miles away from.

So many unpleasant things happen when we do God's work for Him. It also makes us look proud to the man as if we're the only ones that can hear God speak, and we can also get hurt in the process. He resists the proud and gives grace to the humble. Matters of the heart are very sensitive, not to be messed around with, so it's important to guard your heart because from it flows the issues of life.

As adults in waiting for the right timing to meet that soul mate, you shouldn't give your heart to any man in the hope that he will take it on. Don't submit to a man before he decides to marry you. Guard your heart!

Be friends, be pleasant, help in ways that a friend can help, be yourself, but set boundaries where lines are not crossed. When you're clear and focused, you will see who this person is through the friendship; whether he fits into your prayers to God, whether you can live with him, whether he will protect you and be a suitable covering as a husband – all these questions must be asked and answered to your satisfaction before you say I do!

That's not to say you should make your friendship complicated, just be yourself and if he is your soul mate, everything, including questions and clarity in the circumstance, will fall into place. Situations will be orchestrated so that destiny takes precedence. You're submitting to the way God intended to bless you with a partner so that He, not you, will take the glory.

Majority of not waiting in that form is down to lack of patience and trust in what God says He will do. It's when we're not at peace with who we are in God and believing that God will do what He says He will do that we make demands and try hinting to the man that our biological clocks are tick, tick, ticking away.

A woman who is submitted to God prays first about her future partner and that he will find God first in his own circumstances before he finds her, because when he does, he'll know you are his helpmate. This will bring him closer to God to be all that you have prayed for in a man.

I don't know of any godly woman who would like to marry a man who has no passion for God or His business. But from my teenage years, up to the age of about 30 years old, I considered a man who was godly very boring. I didn't think he would know how to please a woman. At the time, to me, a man who was worldly knew every trick in the book and would be able to show me a good time, understand my needs and be very generous in the bedroom department.

Through years and years of dating such men, I realised that most of them were good at showing me what I thought was a good time, but that was always short lived. The excitement leaves and the thirst to keep him interested means having to compromise your own standards and principles, submitting in the wrong way; behaving like the wife without his honouring you by claiming you in public.

Yes, I went through this with ex boyfriends. I realise now that any man who would want to take from you what does not rightfully belong to him is actually robbing you of your virtue as a woman. If submitting to the right man who has honoured you and is your life partner is where your power lies, imagine what submitting to the wrong man under the wrong circumstances can do to you; you become a doormat, a controlled woman whose virtue is being repressed.

We should use Rebekah's single lifestyle as our example of waiting to be found. Even she didn't know what was round the corner when she gave Eliazar and his camel water to drink; she was pure in heart, this enabled her trust in God. She went about doing what she enjoyed doing; and allowed God to do the rest. That trust was reflected when she saw Isaac and covered her face, accepting him as her covering.

Rebekah was young and as such was not thinking along the path of marriage; but there are women who are a lot older than Rebekah was, who struggle to emulate her purity. She was pure in heart; a quality that so many women of a certain age lack.

It's not about concentrating on how beautiful you are as a woman, the amount of money you may have saved up, or the time you spend doing your hair. Even if you're dressed in a sack, your intended partner will see those qualities in you. The reasons these qualities are not apparent in some of us is because of the disappointments, pain, hurt and rejection that has been experienced but hasn't been addressed, so we find it difficult to wait on God. Not waiting on God can actually bring a delay, which the majority of women and men in their mid 30's to late 40's are experiencing.

The frustration of waiting comes from putting a limit on God's timing; and if you've been helping Him, you will end up emotionally tired and drained.

I'm not saying you need to be young like Rebekah because that would be impossible—you can't go back to being 17 years old again, but you can be pure in heart like she was. Such a quality of purity makes you do things without being suspicious or thinking that someone is out to get you. Such a quality enables you to totally trust in God who is looking out for you.

I remember a time when a man would smile at me. It didn't matter who the man was, good or average looking, I would either glare at him in disbelief for having even looked my way or turn away without so much as a smile in response. I felt he was out of his depth to even consider that I would respond in the slightest. Looking back, I realised that I was stroking wounds of disappointment, a broken heart, self-pity and rejection of previous relationships. This is the response we give out, and furthermore, when we start a relationship in that sentiment it's not on the right foundation. We go in with the view that this man is the one who has to stay; we'll make him wipe away the hurt, the tears, the disappointments of the past by offering everything including submission on a plate to him. Not so!

The Day I Met Him

When I eventually met my husband, I was healed from such hurts, disappointments and wounds of the heart. I was whole in me and had nothing to lose because I was at rest in my identity. I had accepted me and all my faults, I wasn't interested in making a false impression on anyone and I didn't feel I had anything to prove. I could wait and I could choose who I wanted to spend the rest of my life with; I wasn't desperate to impress. I had exhaled and was ready to submit to God's choice for me.

I remember that day Tuesday morning at 9.45am. I was sitting under the hairdryer in the local hair salon when this tall, well-built hunk of a man stood in the entrance of the door, blocking out the morning sun which was trying to pierce through. The salon was getting busy as there were women already being attended to and some were also in my position drying their hair with rollers in it.

It was important for me to do my hair that morning as I was invited as a guest speaker for a major conference in another state and was due to catch a domestic flight at 12pm that same day, so I was shuttling with time. I wasn't in the mood to chat; I just needed to get in and out.

I turned my head to find out who was blocking the sunlight and the man gave me a very broad smile, showing all his white teeth.

I looked at him, wondering whether it was me he was smiling at. I looked behind me just to check, thinking it must be someone else and not me. I realised that it was me who had caught his eye and, surprisingly, smiled back at him thinking to myself, 'Here we go, let's see where this takes us.'

My smile must have given him the assurance that it was okay for him to walk up to me, because he came and sat beside me, not minding the glances of the other women in the salon. He said, 'Hi, my name is Frank, what's yours?'

I responded, 'I'm under the drier so I won't be able to hear what you're saying to me.' He smiled again and said, 'That's okay, I'll wait till you're finished.'

But somehow that didn't happen as he continued speaking anyway and I had to take my ear out of the dryer to hear what he was asking me. In that time, I found out that he was an actor, between shoots. I was able to tell him a bit about myself, and that I'm a writer in town to promote my book.

As he handed me his business card, I found myself smiling and thinking to myself, 'I wonder if he's really an actor.'

I surprised myself because I didn't snub him, glare at him or even rudely confront him by telling him he's wasting my time, especially as I was short on time. I was pleasant, smiled, encouraged him to speak and responded by answering him.

I couldn't believe it! I had forgotten about my past pain long enough to allow someone into my space without thinking that the encounter was anything but pleasant. I was myself enough for him to see what he wanted to see—that pure heart without baring all; a rare quality that many disappointed women have hidden.

The Grace to Submit to God

God's grace equips us to do the things we're not able to do in our own strength. His grace aids us to wait for His perfect match in a companion, even though he may not be what we're expecting initially, but through the eyes of Christ, we can see that this person is indeed who God has called us to walk with. It's God's grace that strengthens us as we stand in the gap for our husbands, contending for his spirit to be free to walk in the fullness of his divine purpose, to be the man that God has him to be.

It's the grace of God that enables you to be faithful with His son and as you pray for him to meet God at his point of need, God will send him back to you.

There was a particular period where my friend (the one I believed to be my husband) was going through a period of change with his church. He had been attending this church for close to nine years and he had become so comfortable with the church, he couldn't see himself ever leaving to go somewhere else to worship.

After I joined, things started happening in this church and the circumstances they were going through as a church started speaking to him personally—as a result, it made him minimise his attendance. This man was an elder and to see him not attend a service continuously meant that he was having a change of heart. Of course, I could understand what was happening in that the changes his church was going through stirred up a desire for change in his life, and essentially to change his place of worship.

I remember discussing the issues the church was going through and how it had affected him to the point that he wasn't attending as usual, especially as he held a position of authority in the church. I had also gone through a similar situation in my previous church, which is why I started worshipping at his church.

I told him that he shouldn't allow the issues in church to affect him to the point where he becomes upset or frustrated. The issue is not between he and the church, but rather between him and God; this could be God's way of getting his attention to move with the Holy Spirit and not get entangled with issues of his church.

I encouraged him to go back to God and seek Him diligently for his next direction and he will hear from God concerning this issue.

My approach to him was genuine, which in return made him open to receive everything I had said to him because it was also confirming with him what he already believed in his heart was happening. I believe God was leading him to another level of responsibility and wanted him to be where he can operate in that authority of grace.

After speaking with him, I had an impression in my spirit that God was pleased and it made me understand that when we agree with God and the plans that He has for his sons, and we submit to those plans in being used by God to prayerfully direct His sons to His will for them, then we (women) can also ask whatever we desire according to God's will and He will give it to us. We are called to ask that our joy may be full.

I wanted to see my friend set free and operate in the fulfilment of God's promises and to do this I had to submit to God by sending him back to His Creator—God. I wasn't submitting to my friend who hadn't proposed to me, and we weren't even dating, so I had no business submitting to him even though I thought that we were meant to be married at some point.

This gentleman went back to God for guidance and clarity and he got what he needed—direction.

Submitting the Right Way

The bible instructs wives to submit to our husbands as to the Lord. What does this really mean? There are women who aren't married submitting to their boyfriends and women who are married submitting to their husbands in the wrong way. Submission in the appropriate way is where a woman's power is. Women want to submit to a man who has strength of character and can protect her.

When Rebekah covered herself before Isaac, she was submitting to God's promise in marrying Isaac, which means that she was accepting to be used by God in Isaac's life. This showed her modesty.

When I spoke to my friend to go back to God for clarity and direction regarding the upheaval in his church, I was submitting to God to be used by Him for that particular reason and that was as far as it was meant to go. Just because I believed he was my partner didn't mean that I should submit my role to him when it wasn't time and there was no concrete evidence that he was who God had said was to be my husband.

It is God's responsibility to reveal us to his son. Until then, if you're in a relationship with a man that you believe may be your life partner, continue to agree with God about his destiny whether he may be your husband or not; that's all that is needed for you to do at this point. Being a wife to him before it is time is not submitting in the right way.

God gives us the grace to submit in marriage and in doing so we operate in an authority that creates results. If you're submitting outside of a marriage covenant, then you're submitting outside of the grace of God and in such situations, whoever you submit to becomes lord over you. Imagine another human being who may not know you well, or have the best intentions towards you being your lord—he controls you and such control will never be in your best interest.

If you're in such a relationship, the situation will not change until you apply biblical truth to your situation. Furthermore, a man should count it an honour that he has been chosen to cover and lead you spiritually. Your price is far above rubies!

Spending time in His Presence gives us clarity, it creates an opportunity for us to be intimate with Him; having direction from Him as to what He wants us to do, how He wants us to do it and who He wants us to do it with. If you're single and desire to be married, He requires you to submit to Him first, to have intimacy with Him, because that is what will lead you and keep you in marriage.

God is not in the business of bringing a man and a woman together for the fun of it. He must be satisfied that we are free from emotional ties so that we can be a helpmate to His son; the trials God allows us to go through as single women is to bring forth the 'substance' that His sons are looking for.

It took me close to 10 years to understand that God had answered my desire of being a wife to someone; after all, He put that desire in me, but He was also creating within me the substance that wives have: the ability to create a peaceful home for my husband to come home to, for my children to grow up in the wisdom of the Lord, and to stand in the gap to effect changes in the spiritual realm where my household is concerned. It took 10 years for God to approve me worthy of being a wife to His son. It took 10 years to learn how to submit to God before I could submit to my husband in the right way. And 10 years to realise what tools I had as a helpmate. And when God was satisfied with His work in me He spoke and it made me understand why I had been waiting for the desire to be fulfilled.

On May 6th 2005, as I was meditating and in prayer, He said to me clearly (I can't paraphrase this as the Words He spoke were so unique and special it would be meaningless if paraphrased):

> *For I love you with an everlasting love, before you loved Me, I first loved you. You have been alone so that you will come close to Me; that you may know Me and the Power of My Resurrection.*
>
> *I want you to be intimate with Me. I have not forsaken you; I only wanted you to know Me more and more. I have not forgotten you. I kept you on your own that you may come closer to Me. This is what most people miss; intimacy with Me. I have not forgotten you, I never have. I have done all of this for you to have a close fellowship with Me.*

At that moment the voice was so strong within me, the desire to be married was no longer there, all I wanted was God; it didn't matter that I was still single. I also realised that God had not forgotten my desire for marriage. He wanted me to know Him intimately because that is what would keep me in marriage. In the tough times, the times that I may feel like giving up because my husband is not with me spiritually or emotionally, because he doesn't 'understand' me; when circumstances become too much to bear, the knowledge of who God is to me is what would keep me and give me hope to continue in the tough seasons. This is what it means to submit in the right way. To stay where God has called me and who He has called me to be with, despite issues that may arise to attack the union. God's grace is most definitely our support during such times.

Women (myself included) have the tendency to think with our hearts; so we're prone to loving a man easily without seeing the flaws (and we all have them). Our heart will override our head, and that is why we must learn to run to God's covering first before the covering of a man (Ezekiel 16: 7—8).

The love we have inside must first be showered on God before it goes to a potential husband.

I have seen cases where a potential relationship between a man and a woman has dissolved because the foundation in which they are together is not based on the truth. Either the woman is looking to the man to fulfil certain areas in her life and the man looking to the woman to help him in ways that may compromise her position as a woman.

Our relationship with God teaches us how to submit and not compromise our positions of authority in the spiritual realm, even in our marriage. He encourages us to come to Him first, thereby not looking to the man to make the impossible possible. After all, he's not superman; he's flesh and blood with needs of his own.

As we run to God, wisdom reveals to us what resources we have to help our future husband. We may not know all that we have, but it will be enough to start with.

When I was single I spent so much time discussing and asking

God why I was still single. I did whatever I believed the Holy Spirit was leading me to do including opening two businesses and closing them, and preparing myself in ways that I believed God wanted me to be, so I was ready for that man.

I spent most of my time learning to understand God's plan for my life to the point where I wanted to understand God's plan for marriage and how He would bless me to be fruitful in that way. Men admire women who are focused and know what they want. Your drive and enthusiasm for the things of God will most certainly stir him up as a famous biblical quote says, 'iron sharpens iron'.

Submitting the Wrong Way

It's important to note that God is Love — everything He does is out of love for us. Therefore, His blessing you is because He loves you and wants you to receive His way. The mistake that most single Christian women often make is to look for a man who they will fall in love with; someone who will rock their world. If you ask them to describe who this person would be it would be tall, dark, handsome, well dressed and so forth. The enemy knows this so he will entice us with such men in dreams where we will think that this must be 'my husband', and most times through the course of time, it turns out to be the deception of our souls.

I remember going to church and believing that I would find my husband in church – and take note of the statement, 'I would find him', not him finding me. I was on a quest to meet this man who God had prepared for me.

I was also deceived into thinking that a particular gentleman was indeed my husband and I was waiting for God to reveal this to him so that he could propose. My prayers were based on him catching the revelation that I believed God had given me.

I would join his social networks because I was under the illusion that I needed to see how he was with his friends. I took an interest in his recreational activities. This continued for five years because

I believed he was my husband; and for five years I would have confirming dreams that he will catch the revelation and soon we would be husband and wife. Eventually, when he told me that he couldn't give me what I needed, I started to ponder on my dreams and how none of them had come to pass. I was living in my own deception, until I came across a passage that explained a lot more:

> 'The prophet who has a dream, let him tell his dream; but he who has My word, let him speak My word faithfully. What has straw in common with wheat?
>
> Is not My Word like fire (that consumes all that cannot endure the test)? says the Lord, and like a hammer that breaks in pieces the rock (of most stubborn resistance)? Jeremiah 23:28/29

The Word would test my dreams and expose the deception of the dreams. And to know the Word is to spend time in it. In doing so, I realised these dreams were to keep me out of my destiny, waiting for someone who was never for me. I also realised that my prayers towards this man were not honourable. They were self-centred, ambitious prayers (see James 3:14-17).

When my husband found me, I didn't go weak at the knees or the sound of my heart beating so fast. This wasn't an infatuated feeling. This doesn't mean that I didn't love him as I ought to, but I was more in love with God and wanted to do His Will. I was settled in my spirit and had entered into my rest where this desire was concerned. Meeting him was just another ordinary day. The clouds didn't erupt and the heavens didn't open either. It was a peaceful day on my way to a speaking engagement.

I was focused and I didn't recognise him to be my husband – not that he isn't a very attractive man. My focus was more on do-ing God's will. I even remembered telling him during one of our many interesting conversations that I wasn't desperate. He looked at me with a look that said 'Where have you been all my life'. I was at peace with who I was. All the trials, the struggles, the pain, the rejection I experienced in life had brought me to a place of acceptance and stillness, ready to move ahead with God whether I was married or not; I wanted His perfect will.

Rebekah didn't know Isaac; she knew God. Eliazar saw in Rebekah the qualities that Abraham spoke of and knew this was a woman suitable to submit to the will of God in her life. Rebekah also knew what to do because her heart was pure. So pure that she knew Eliazar's camel also needed water.

When we submit to God's will in the right way, everything connected to us comes into order. He upholds His will in your life; however, if we try to make things work our way, we'll be spending time upholding what we tried to make happen in our own strength.

Testimonies of Women who Submitted the Right Way

> 'I prayed beforehand that I didn't want more than one suitor; I knew that God would choose who would be right for me. Before I met him, I had come to a peace with God regarding marriage; I wasn't anxious any longer. I didn't have to run after him, I was whole in my spirit to submit to God's will for my life where my partner was concerned.' *Nana*

> 'I wasn't passionately in love, I felt that God gave me an opportunity to be confident with who I was; if there was something wrong with this man then I was happy to know that it would flag up in time, because I wasn't in a rush. I was chosen on my terms. My relationship with God made me confident in myself and I wasn't going to compromise that for anyone. His approach was also different, he was very respectful of me and my mother.' *Saleah*

" '‎I had given up seeking for a man to marry me; I wanted God's will and He gave me a scripture— Ephesians 5:25. This gave me peace about who my husband is and when he will find me. What I hadn't realised at the time was the man that I had known for close to two years was the man God had chosen as my husband. I couldn't see it because I had an image of who I wanted as my husband and I was seeking for that image not realising that I had created an idol in my heart. Once I got rid of the idol I was able to see this man and God's will for me in his life.' *Lynda*

In my experience, and through discussions with my male friends, I have come to realise that men don't enjoy being pressured into a commitment; a man who is confident in his abilities as a man would prefer to seek for his wife through the Holy Spirit. And sure enough, he knows what he is looking for in a wife. Not a girl-friend— but a wife (Proverbs 19:14).

That's okay, open your eyes to his mistakes, question his flaws; he's not perfect just like you; all he needs is a helpmate able to accept him without you thinking that every flaw or mistake revealed is evidence that he is out to take advantage of you.

Know what you're getting into. At this time of your life, you can't go in with your head in the clouds and butterflies in your heart. Understand his character and have confidence in the fact that if he is your mate, God has equipped you for the years you have together. And what you have in you is good enough to bring him into the great man he is called to be.

Wherever you are in the world, God's power through His Spirit is able to connect you to the man He has prepared as your husband. To be found by such a man, means you must be submitted to God in the right way: spirit, soul and body. When you understand the principle and the power you have as a woman, when you submit to God and His way, it doesn't matter where you are in the world, your steps will be ordered to where your husband will find you.

God loves you enough to give you the best, therefore it is important not to miss the opportunity of making the transition from single status to marriage. We've all had the relationships where you meet this man for the first time, you can't believe he likes you the way you like him; every time you see him you're gone with your emotions; you don't see his mistakes, his flaws and so on. You think he's the best thing that you've ever come across.

Yes, it's happened to all of us. And it has gotten most of us into trouble. But God loves you too much to leave you to go into a marriage relationship that way. He wants you to go in with the understanding and the spiritual sense developed in you through the processes of life.

How Rebekah's Role Depicted Fulfilling Purpose

When Rebekah followed Eliazar back to Isaac to assume her role as his wife, the long journey wouldn't have been easy. Perhaps there were some doubts, perhaps the road was rough, perhaps there were discouragements, but they didn't deter her commitment. This was her purpose and no matter the process to reaching it, she wasn't going to give it to anyone. She dismounted the camel as a sign of respect, and she veiled herself as a sign of modesty.

Rebekah walked by faith, called out of her world, looking for a husband. This marriage typifies the church that walks by faith: in the world though not of the world, waiting for her bridegroom, Christ. Isaac went out to meet Rebekah and bring her home; the Lord Jesus will come to bring His bride, the Church, home.

There were no miracles in this union, only God's sovereign programme being carried out.

A worthy wife is a crown for her husband,
but a disgraceful woman is like cancer in his bones.

Proverbs 12:4 NLT

Reflection Time

CASE STUDY

Meet Janet. She has been a Christian for the past nine years, has a strong faith in God, and believes that one day He will bless her with a suitable man who will love her for who she is.

Janet is an experienced image consultant and takes on a professional sculptor as a client. She changes his image, develops his social network and advises him to extend his style of sculpturing to raise his profile. She also sets up an office for him with staff to support the daily business demands. She establishes his business.

Eventually they start a romantic relationship, which becomes quite incestuous (being so close or intimate as to prevent proper functioning). He becomes possessive and demanding, preventing her from seeing her friends. She has fallen in love with him and can't bring herself to stop the relationship even though they constantly argue. She believes she received a spiritual revelation of this man's calling and that he came at a time when she was praying for her husband.

However, after two years in the relationship, feeling that it is taking her away from her relationship with God, Janet breaks up with the sculptor to focus all her attention in redeveloping her faith.

The separation made her reflective but left her also missing him. Janet still believes that the sculptor is her husband and, after a short break, starts seeing him again.

Let's say Janet is your friend, and she comes to you because she needs you to advise her about her situation.

How would you advise Janet?

CHAPTER FIVE

Men Need Their Own Revelation to Love

5

Men Need their Own Revelation to Love

'I HAVE NOTHING TO GIVE YOU.'

THIS was what he told me over dinner one evening. He took me out for a wonderful meal, lovely restaurant, the whole works. This is it... I thought. He was going to propose. We had known each other for close to five years and I had been waiting for him to tell me that he knows... he knows that I am his wife, he's known for a while, but wasn't quite sure how I would take it if he told me immediately. I was so happy and could hardly wait to see the ring. Maybe he'd present it to me in the wine glass, I thought as I took a sip; that's where I'd find it, in the wine glass.

Well to my utter dismay and surprise, he told me how he really felt. He had nothing to give me.

I looked at him waiting for him to explain what he meant by the statement, but no explanation came forth. It was as if he expected me to understand what he meant and take it as final. I looked at him, into his eyes searching for a glimmer of hope that he may be cracking a joke before he presents the ring, but his face was as serious as a judge, his eyes looking straight into mine, showing me that he was not joking, he was serious.

There was an unsettled silence between us. I wanted the ground to open up and swallow me whole. At the same time I had so many questions like... 'Why did you to take me out to tell me this?' 'Didn't you think to just inform me on the phone?' and 'Why did it take you this long to tell me? Five years – are you that callous?'

I had so much turmoil in me and at the same time I had this unexplained peace; at least I knew where he stood, I thought to myself. How much worse could my life get. If the man I thought I knew was my husband is not the person, then who is it?

On the ride home, I felt lonely, empty and crushed, and all I wanted to do was go home and hide. Furthermore, I kept pondering on his statement, that he had nothing to give me; what did that mean? What did it really mean?

The ride home was a long silent one. This person didn't think to find out how I was feeling and I wasn't prepared to offer him a description of my condition.

After saying goodnight, I went up to my flat and sat down and for the first time I had nothing to lean on, no crutch. All my crutches had been taken away, the job, the promise of a thriving business. I willingly let go because I thought I had this guy, I thought my life was changing because I was soon to be married and in my mind, letting go was part of the preparation to move to a new life with my husband. So in practical terms, I had nothing. I was alone and I felt an emptiness which was beyond words. As I went on my knees in humility, I called to God to hold me because I had nothing. After a brief silence, I heard in my inner man, you're not alone, you have Me. I knew that God understood my pain and immediately those words made me understand that God had a bigger plan for my life.

Looking back, I realised that this man wasn't emotionally ready for me, he had nothing to give me. Even though he was comfortable, money wasn't an issue for him, he was gainfully employed and was building a business in property so money wasn't what he couldn't give me. What he couldn't give me was himself, he wasn't emotionally ready to commit and looking back I now know that I would have been looking after him emotionally, which would take me off track and see me concentrating on him for the rest of my life. I would always be babysitting him, wondering what he's up to when he's not with me —a very unhealthy position for a woman to be in and I know I deserve more.

In my mind, I was in a limiting place because everything around me was stagnant, even the book I had written was waiting for me to do something with it and I didn't have the confidence to take it to the next level of development. But the moment we parted ways, I seemed to have so many ideas that I wanted to run with. I could see my purpose. I realised that this man had been used in my life to bring me to a place in my heart ready to receive the man God had prepared for me.

Women need emotional stability; it doesn't matter if he is financially buoyant or academically qualified, that can change overtime, but if he is not emotionally ready to be a husband he will fail you and you will always find yourself lacking that foundation that a man gives as a husband for a wife to blossom and be the person she's called to be.

A man who is prepared will know the kind of wife he needs to help him build. The Holy Spirit would have given him a vision, a desire of the wife and for such to happen, he needs to be in the right place; a place that will help him progress and build.

I've heard people say he needs to have a home, a car, an education, money in the bank—all relevant but conditional. These conditional criteria do not apply when God is uniting a match based on purpose. Such acquisitions can be achieved in partnership with your helpmate.

But a man whom God has prepared to walk into purpose will submit to God's plans for his life and if that means that a particular woman God has chosen will do this, he will answer the call. Why do you think Isaac readily accepted Rebekah when he saw her? He had never seen nor met Rebekah before she presented herself to him in the field.

Major Events Can Change Your Focus

Meanwhile, Isaac, whose home was in the Negev, had returned from Beer-lahai-roi. One evening as he was walking and meditating in the fields, he looked up and saw the camels coming.

When Rebekah looked up and saw Isaac she quickly dismounted from her camel. 'Who is that man walking through the fields to meet us?' she asked the servant. And he replied, 'It is my master.' Rebekah covered her face with her veil, then the servant told Isaac everything he had done.

Rebekah covered her face with her veil, then the servant told Isaac everything he had done, and he accepted Rebekah as his wife and he loved her dearly. He had found a companion in Rebekah who would comfort him where he wouldn't grieve over his mother's passing any longer. He was no longer alone.[1]

We know that in a few chapters back, Sarah, Isaac's mother, had died. We are told that Abraham went to mourn and weep for Sarah and as he was a foreigner in the land she died, he had to ask for property for a burial place where he could bury his wife (Genesis 23: 2, 4).

I'm sure that if it affected Abraham, it must have affected Isaac more. Sarah's death must have left a void in Isaac's heart. Unless you've been through a bereavement, grief is a very personal emotion. The death of a loved one can alter the way one views life and if there isn't a close relationship with God, they could be grieving for many years. I know people who have grieved for the loss of a loved one for over 10 years.

---

1   *Scripture Reference Genesis 24:62-67*

At the same time Rebekah was getting ready for her journey to meet Isaac; Isaac was also going through major changes in his own life.

Now Isaac had returned from going to the well Beer-lahai-roi, for he now dwelt in the south country (The Negev).

Sarah's death must have changed Isaac's focus and as a result he needed something that could give him the meaning of life, his purpose, the reason for his being. Those who have experienced death of a loved one tend to think along these lines… the meaning of life.

We are told that Isaac had returned from Beer-lahai-roi. We hear about this place when the angel of Lord had spoken to Hagar, Sarai's maid, and told her events that would unfold in her life.

So she called the name of the Lord who spoke to her, 'You are the God of seeing', for she said, 'Have I not even here (in the wilderness) looked upon Him Who sees me (and lived)? Or have I here also seen the (future purposes or designs of) Him who sees me?'

Therefore the well was called Beer-lahai-roi (A well to the Living One who sees me); it is between Kadesh and Bered. (Genesis 16: 13-14)

Let's look deeper into that location Beer-lahai-roi. Genesis 16: 13 explains the name as a result of Hagar crying out: 'Even here have I looked after the One seeing me!' The whole compound carries a myriad of meanings: The Declaration That Makes Life Visible; The Explanation That Shows The Image Of Life; The Well Of Life Vision, or Of The Life That Sees; or Sees Me.

> NOTE:
>
> *The name Beer-lahai-roi is a composite consisting of four segments: (1) The Hebrew verb (ba'ar) declare, make plain, with its derivative be'er, meaning well, pit. The Old Testament states that the derivative is uncertain, but the many obvious relations between springs of water and springs of revelation may provide hints of clarity. (2) The Hebrew particle (le) which denotes direction, position, relation or possession. In this case, the letter denotes relation or even possession. (3) The Hebrew adjective (hay) meaning living. Sometimes it is used to mean kinsfolk/family, as in 1 Samuel 18:18. (4) The Hebrew verb (raa) meaning to see, look at, and, much as in English, came to serve meanings such as understand (Aha, I see...). The final word in our name can be the third person of the verb (he sees), but is also identical to the noun that means appearance and even mirror.*

Most times we don't understand the meaning of life until a major event is experienced. Such events (bereavement, separation, relocation, major accidents, relationships etc.) can bring a change of mind set and introduce us to our life's purpose. It creates an opening where we search for the reason for our being and in most cases people want a personal encounter with God. They want to know that their life has a meaning on earth.

I believe that the death of his mother led Isaac to seek God's face for direction, so he went to Beer-lahai-roi to hear from the 'One who Sees Me'; to obtain specific direction. We know that Abraham and his family were living in Canaan, until the death of Sarah. Maybe the loss of his mother had brought a loneliness to Isaac that it caused him to seek God. It could have been on this trip that God had prepared Isaac for a change of direction in his own life, because on his return, he had moved from Canaan to the south country called The Negev.

> *NOTE:*
>
> *We are told that The Negev, which extends over Israel's southern region, accounts for over half of Israeli's land area. Due to its desert character, however, this region is sparsely populated.*
>
> *Today, The Negev has seen its share of history. Abraham built his home in Be'er Sheva, the Nabateans passed through there on caravans of camels laden with precious trade goods. For these and other reasons, the Negev has become one of Israeli's popular tourism sites.*

Isaac had moved to what seemed like a deserted location to the naked eyes. However, it didn't matter, his total trust and surrendering to God to move to a new location was an opportunity for him to be fruitful.

Relocating for Purpose

Location means a lot to God. It's important to know where you're meant to operate from. I believe that when you're in the right location, everything you need to develop or build is available to you in that location. The same applies for the church you attend. The word you need to grow and build is most times available to you in the church you've been led to worship in.

Isaac's location in The Negev was where he was called to build from— his starting point.

During my single season, I heard men say that they want to be prepared before they get married. The kind of preparation they talk about is the physical preparation: a house, a car, a good job earning millions. There's nothing wrong with this picture, only that it ignores the need for men to be also emotionally and spiritually prepared.

Most times the search for material acquisitions can take years and years, in doing so, men miss the point at which they ought to be taking a wife.

What seems like a good idea to get married now becomes a complicated issue because when a man gets to a certain age, he depends so much on his material acquisitions that he doesn't trust any woman to permanently build with him.

Such men start with a 'let's see how it goes' kind of friendship, and before the woman knows it five years on and they're still seeing how it's going with no clear plans to make it legal.

I remember a friend who was also waiting for the right mate to come along and make it permanent. She met someone who was 50 years old, had never been married, had no children, and before you say it, no not gay either—seemed like a dream, right? Well, what was wrong with this picture was that he could never see himself getting married and she found this out after praying about him. Prayer, always a wise choice, reveals the hidden things; the things we can't see or understand. Ten years on and he's still not married.

As I said before, there is nothing wrong with preparing yourself, but the preparation has to be in line with God's plans and purpose for your life and the woman who will share it with you. Men, you have to prepare to make room for her when you find her.

This doesn't mean that you should put your life on hold; I mean, it's important for God to prepare you for the woman He has chosen for His son, only the Holy Spirit knows what you need and how you can get it.

God was preparing Isaac in spite of what Isaac was doing. The loss of his mother, the seeking God for direction, the relocation and the place where he was meditating in the fields, were all preparation. Others may see that he was in an isolated place, but it was a place that made him sure of who God was to him, to receive instructions for his new life.

Every man who wants a wife needs this time with God. It's a place of humility, a place of spiritual positioning, a place of spiritual understanding, a place of total dependency on God and His promises for you. He may not know everything (like the fictional superman character who sports himself to be superhuman conquering the bad guy and winning the heart of the lead woman), but he knows God enough to know that this is the time he needs a wife who is going to be a suitable companion and help mate to him. Therefore his choice is based on God's choice for him.

If you're a man reading this and you've been in that place of fear to move forward, God wants you to trust in Him and His promises to you about your help mate.

Unbeknownst to Isaac, God was preparing him for his destiny as a spiritual leader, a husband, a father, a covering, a provider. A man who will not walk out when the going gets tough, a man who will discern the Spirit of wisdom in his wife. A man who will not take for granted that his woman will be submitting to him as unto the Lord.

A man who will learn how to love his wife as Christ loves the Church. This kind of preparation teaches a man to be emotionally ready to marry and to love even when it hurts. It's unconditional, it's selfless and it's through God.

Please don't misunderstand me, this type of man cannot do the above in his flesh, he realises his weaknesses and as such is ready to depend on God to learn how to be responsible in marriage. This is a man who is operating in purpose.

The Epitome of His Vision
One of the many ideas I had took me to another country. I packed up everything ready to move to where God would use me.

There was nothing keeping me in England; the man who I thought would be 'the one' wasn't. I had published my book and my eyes could see beyond where I was, I could use my skills in any country that I wanted to live and I was going to use them in Nigeria.

Even though I'm originally Nigerian, I hadn't been back for over 18 years so my journey to Nigeria was one of apprehension and uncertainty, yet filled with excitement as to why the Holy Spirit was leading me to Nigeria.

Exciting because I could start building with my newly found and developed skills in writing, speaking and teaching. At this point I wasn't looking to get married any longer. I figured that since I got it wrong with the last person, I didn't want to make anymore assumptions, besides it was easier having a companion in the Holy Spirit, because He loved me for who I am, I didn't have to pretend or impress Him.

Little did I know that God had other plans.

I met my husband on an ordinary day, no earth shattering noises, the heavens didn't open and God spoke; it was simply an ordinary day. I was invited to speak at a conference and I needed to prepare for this conference and part of the preparation was to go to the hairdresser's to get my hair done.

On spotting me he came in whilst I was under the hairdryer. Imagine a beauty place full of women and this tall, well-built man comes in with a smile directed at me. I thought to myself, who is he smiling at. With that warm smile he came over to sit next to me and the rest is history.

He'd seen me before I laid eyes on him and in spotting me, according to his side of events, he knew that his search was over. He had found his wife.

Through our friendship (not dating), just friends, I got to know so much about this man. He was a Nollywood actor who had come to a point in his life where acting was no longer for him. He felt he had to choose between his career and the immoral demands it can bring or his relationship with Christ and safeguard his principles, values and beliefs. He chose to leave the industry and wait for direction.

Just like Isaac, he had relocated and was spending more time meditating on God waiting for direction. He was in the process of relocating to Canada, then I came along. I was an answer to his prayer of direction. He had been praying for help, and he finds me (laughs).

Men like to feel that they can take care of things. They're so busy chasing security, they can miss a move of God in their life and the preparation needed to get them ready for a season of increase. I believe they were created this way, however, when a man feels that he can take care of things without God, it's difficult for him to see what God wants him to see until he comes to the end of himself; only then is he able to listen out for God's guidance.

Only then will he submit to his purpose and the gift in the woman that is connected to his purpose; only then can he give himself to a woman and love her as he loves himself; only then will he be able to protect her and support her emotionally.

When my husband saw me, he knew who I would be to him – after all, he was in a place of expectancy. I was the one who didn't know. I was engrossed in what I went to Nigeria to do, so wasn't looking for anyone to come into my life at that point.

It's like God took my mind off the fact that I wanted to be married, made me concentrate on something else, and then slipped this man before me. And when he started to show so much interest in me, I found myself going back to God to ask Him who Frank was.

With every question I asked God about Frank, every time we met, Frank would answer the questions I had already asked God.

I was asked to speak at a singles' conference and at the time Frank had already made his intentions clear to me. Most of the women at the conference wanted to hear from Frank and how he knew that I was his wife. In answering, he described me as the epitome of his vision, and said that he wanted to build his life around me.

He Can Only Love When He Knows God's Love
The discussions I've had with men, including my own brothers and my husband, makes me realise that men suffer different forms of rejection and pain. This is not to say that women don't experience the same, because they do too. But when a man suffers rejection, pain, emotional trauma and above all loneliness, they find it hard to confide in other men.

Most men in general find it hard to communicate their inner feelings to anyone, hence most of them grow up with hidden scars of their past. Growing up, they're taught not to cry, but to be a man! As a result, such scars become barriers to their progress when they're older. That boy who was abused is still locked away in his inner person and the only person that can take that away and re-place it with love is God. As spiritual leaders, these men become a target for the enemy. If he can take them out, then the family unit becomes unbalanced because the man is the head of the home and his role as a spiritual leader is also crucial to the nurturing of that home.

Hurting people hurt other people and this statement definitely ap-plies to men who've grown up with wounds so deep, it would prob-ably take a lifetime for any emotional healing to be evident.

As women, we deal with the brunt of their pain, the infidelity, abuse, lies, disloyalty, absenteeism, rejection; all are symptoms of a man's pain.

Such men need to be re-taught how to love themselves before they can ever think of loving someone else. As I mentioned at the be-ginning of this chapter, such a man will have nothing to offer you. It doesn't mean their hearts are not sensitive, in fact it's the op-posite; their hearts are very sensitive, however they may not know how to deal with their hurt and as such transfer it to someone else.

God's love draws a man who has come to the end of himself into His Presence so that He can take away the hurt, clear the hidden tears and strengthen him emotionally to love someone else. God's love for this man translates in the form of a wife who will be a companion to him, protect him, cover his back and spiritually stand against any evil lurking around to attack him.

God's love does this and a man who experiences this kind of heal-ing and wholeness has a revelation of what His love has done for him and as a result is able to love a woman, love her—not hurt her.

Yes, God knows what His sons need and He prepares a woman to represent this love once He has prepared him to love this woman.

And when he finds a woman, he will define who she is to him. When Eve was brought to Adam, he was able to claim her and define who she was to him – at last, the man exclaimed, 'This is bone from my bone and flesh from my flesh! She will be called woman, because she was taken from man.'

Such a man will know why you've been brought to him and will not take the friendship for granted in an ungodly way. And a woman who knows what she wants will not allow her emotions to be taken for granted by a man who doesn't know what he wants. She won't compromise her principles just to make him happy. A man who knows the love of God will never ask that from her.

When my husband found me, he knew who I would become to him, he knew that I was his wife and although he didn't tell me his discovery immediately, our blossomed friendship confirmed his thoughts that I was definitely his wife.

When he eventually told me, he defined what he wanted from me; I didn't have to ask him, he defined it! It was left to me to either accept or not accept.

My point is that a man who has come to that point of submission in God will never leave you hanging on; he loves God too much for that to happen.

When a man reaches this point, then and only then through the eyes of Christ and with the help of the Holy Spirit will he find his wife.

He'll also understand what he needs and the resources she has to complement him to achieve and how his role as her spiritual covering is crucial to her development.

A man who humbly submits to the Spirit of wisdom in his wife is a man walking in purpose and such a man who has found such a woman, finds a good thing and obtains favour from the Lord.

How Isaac's Role Depicted Fulfilling Purpose

Abraham was to become a mighty nation through his son Isaac. Obviously Isaac must have children, and this necessitated a wife.

Since his offspring would need to be faithful to God and to keep His covenant, the wife would need to be a godly woman. This implied that she could not be a Canaanite. Also, since God had promised 'this land', Isaac must not return to Mesopotamia. Isaac needed a wife because he must become a husband and father to fulfil his part in the outworking of the Abrahamic covenant.

While it is the norm for men to marry, let us not forget that the bible informs us that it is also sometimes God's purpose to keep some of His servants single. In my opinion, marriage should only be sought for those who will achieve God's purpose by having a mate and, perhaps, a family. You may beg to differ in that opinion, but that's okay.

The will of God was discerned through prayer. The servant submitted a plan to God whereby the woman who was to be Isaac's wife would become evident.

This was no fleece but rather a test of character. The servant could thereby determine the character of the women he would meet. God providentially (through circumstances) brought the right woman to the servant, and by her generous act of watering the camels she evidenced that she was His choice for Isaac's wife.

*There are three things that amaze me— no, four
things that I don't understand. How an eagle
glides through the sky, how a snake slithers on a
rock, how a ship navigates the ocean and how a
man loves a woman.*

Proverbs 30:18-19 NLT

Reflection Time

CASE STUDY

Joseph had completed his final year in psychology. Finding a job wasn't easy and as such he felt discouraged and resentful that his years in university had not resulted in one successful job application in three years.

His emotional state directed him to church where he spent the better part of his time, whilst others were out working. If he wasn't in the church then he would be socialising with his friends over a much needed drink.

Being raised in a close loving family in a rural part of Africa, he would follow in the steps of his older siblings, which is to marry once he's settled (job, house, car etc).

One day in church, Joseph meets a lady who happened to be visiting from another state. They start a discussion and immediately hit it off as friends.

This young woman is very established and wealthy, with about six plots of land, two rental properties and three cars. He soon starts to enjoy the gifts she gives him (Blackberry handset, top ups for his phones, and the promise to pay for his journey to her state etc).

They soon become intimate and their many deep conversations leads to the preparation of a wedding. Even though they don't live in the same state, they know they love each other.

Joseph's older brother is very weary of this union as he feels that Joseph hasn't really got himself settled with some form of stable job to generate an income for his welfare and establish himself as a provider.

He doesn't have anything against the woman; he simply doesn't want his brother to go into a permanent relationship without having his own footing, and a source of income to look after his wife. He also believes that she could control him in the marriage because she is established and he isn't.

Do you think Joseph's older brother is right in his opinions?

If you were in Joseph's shoes how would you take this relationship further?

CHAPTER SIX

Be Ready, Get Into Position and Receive!

6

Be Ready, Get Into Position and Receive!

———— ⊙⌒⌒⊙ ————

THERE'S nothing worse than an opportunity coming your way and you're not prepared for it.

Think back to a time when an opportunity was presented to you and you didn't know what to do with it. A likely result is that somebody else benefited from it. How did it make you feel?

When I was single, I had an idea of the kind of man I wanted to marry (this also included his culture, outlook and so many other factors that I had listed). I didn't want to marry a Nigerian, as I believed that I would not get along with Nigerian men. Even though I am from Nigerian descent, my outlook was different from a culturally based Nigerian. Furthermore I wasn't very domesticated as Nigerian men would like for me to be. I am not the kind of woman to have dinner ready when I've also been working. I expect him to do his share of looking after the children when we have them and above all support me in my endeavours as I would with him. Somehow I couldn't see a Nigerian man having such qualities and furthermore not one whose base is in Nigeria.

Well, I was totally wrong to have conjured such stereotypical beliefs in my mind. Funnily enough, my father wasn't like the men I had imagined African men to be like, he was very much the opposite, and I would have wanted someone like him. However, I had heard of stories from friends and family about how difficult African men are, especially from my own country—Nigeria, and based on their own negative experiences, I decided that I didn't want to be in their shoes.

How wrong I was. It was purpose that took me back to Africa—Nigeria, a place I hadn't visited for over 20 years and that was where I met my husband—Frank.

My stereotypical views of African men prevented me from praying according to God's will for my life. I seemed to be praying out of fear as opposed to faith. However, God understood the fear I had in my heart and took me through a process of developing my faith, where it didn't matter what I felt as long as I was doing what God wanted me to do; as long as I was pleasing Him, then I would go to the ends of the earth for Him; as long as He called me to do then I would do it.

This peace of mind didn't happen over night. The process to submitting to His will took me through a few mountain and valley experiences so that I could move in His leading and as such be blessed with the desires of my heart—my husband.

I guess when I communicated to God about marriage 10 years before I actually got married, I wasn't ready to receive God's best for me, coupled with the fact that God's best for me had to also be part of my purpose.

At the time, my conversations to God would go like this: 'God, wherever my husband is in the world, bring him to me. If he is sleeping wake him up, if he is near, open his spiritual eyes to behold his wife.'

As I write this I laugh because it seemed like I was saying that I'm in position, ready to receive, but there seems to be a problem with whoever this man is so God would have to get him in location.

In fact, I was the one that was being prepared to get into position to receive. He could have also been working on Frank, but how would I have known that when we were not even in the same country? Looking back I can now see that God's provision was based on timing, preparation and positioning.

There is Provision for Every Need

I am a great believer that every need we have is provided for by God in Christ Jesus. This is confirmed by a verse that tells us that God provides our needs according to His riches in glory in Christ Jesus – Philippians 4:19.

Provision is simply providence for a vision. Therefore, needs are not only limited to financial. There are so many needs in the world we live in and such needs have been fuelled by a desire, a genuine desire put there by God. So He gives us a desire that He's already provided for.

Most times we may not know where to look for the provision or better still obtain the provision we need to fulfil our desire.

It's not our duty to worry about provision, that's God's duty and only when you're in an intimate relationship with Christ, will you receive His provision for the vision that He has given you.

God's providence is already in position; you're responsibility is to seek for it through Christ. The 'seeking' is the process that brings you to maturity, perfect timing and the right location to receive the providence for your need.

As human beings, we worry so much about provision. Some

are concerned to leave their jobs to start a new venture because they have no idea where provision will come from; some are frightened to marry because they don't have the provision for their ceremony.

Time is spent worrying due to this one main thing, 'provision', and yet this one thing has already been taken care of by the Provider of the vision.

I guarantee you that whatever vision you have, be it marriage, business, ministry, projects, as long as it's in line with God's purpose for you, there is already provision for your vision. The process to finding the provision is how trusting you are in the Provider.

However, like I said, provision is not limited to money. You must be ready to receive what provision God gives you for your vision. His provision will always come in seed form.

Here are some examples of people who were ready to receive God's provision:

ABRAHAM—was instructed by God to take his only son and sacrifice him. On getting to Mount Moriah, God provided him with a ram for the sacrifice. Most bible scholars explain that Abraham believed God that he would raise Isaac from the dead.

ELIJAH— after defeating the 400 prophets of Baal, Elijah was on the run from Jezebel. God instructed him to go to Brook Kerith where he would drink from the brook and eat what the ravens brought him. When the brook dried up, God had provided provision for him with the widow of Zarephath.

RUTH—after the death of her husband, Ruth followed Naomi back to Bethlehem. On Naomi's instruction, Ruth went to work on Boaz's field where she was able to pick up left over grain that had been harvested. Boaz liked her so much that he looked after her whilst she was working in the field. During lunchtime Boaz would offer her food and water to drink. The story ends when Boaz marries her.

ADAM—looked too lonely, and every animal he was given and named wasn't a compatible helper for him. God provided a helpmate in the form of Eve and when Adam saw her, he received her with open arms.

REBEKAH—our main story tells us that Eliazar prayed for God to lead him to the right woman for Isaac, and when he came to the well he found Rebekah. That was also proven when she offered him water for his camel. I strongly believe that Rebekah was positioned at the well for Eliazar to see her.

These people were ready, they were in position and received the provision for their vision. God's providence is already in position. He is dealing with us to break down the limitations in our mind to receive what He knows we need for the vision He has given us. We demonstrate that we're ready when we follow His Spirit into position to receive.

For so long I'd always believed that my life partner was already in England. If not England, then it must be America. I never thought that he would be in Nigeria. It never crossed my mind; partly because I had no intentions of visiting Nigeria and also because I couldn't see myself marrying a Nigerian— as I believed they were too cultural and traditional in their thinking and I was broadminded and didn't need to be controlled by someone else's ideals.

I was very wrong in my thinking and my mindset was limiting me from being blessed, from being ready, being in position and receiving from God.

The funny thing is that I really believed that my thoughts were right and that due to my beliefs God would bless me.

It was only through my experiences of life, lessons of humility (waiting can also humble you), being chastised, that my thoughts were being exposed as stereotypes. What you believe and act on can either make you fruitful or keep you in a stagnant place.

My prayers regarding this topic was based on God giving me a mate that I thought would complement me. I wasn't praying according to God's purpose for me, I was praying according to my own desires and my own fear. Fear that a man from Nigeria would not allow me to be who God wanted me to be, fear based on stories that I'd heard about men from that culture, and as such I was blocking out God's will for my life. How could I receive what I feared?

I attended over 50 weddings of close friends and family in the space of 10 years and didn't think much of it. I would go home wondering when my wedding would happen and thoughts of my wedding dress and how the occasion would pan out.

I started to realise that there was a problem when my inner circle of friends were getting married. I was a bridesmaid at a very close friend's wedding along with another person, and the second bridesmaid even met her husband during the period that we were preparing for our friend's wedding.

I started to think, this isn't a coincidence; there is something I'm missing. It was when my youngest sister, the last born of our family, announced her wedding date and she wanted me to become a bridesmaid (I declined and offered to do a reading instead) that got me thinking that I must have passed my sell-by date in the marriage department (jokingly).

I thought that God had forgotten me since as the first child of five I was still single, but the third, fourth and now fifth child were all married. They were not 'shot gun' marriages; they all married good mates and it got me pondering whether I was in the right position to hear and receive.

Don't get me wrong, where purpose is concerned, everyone has their own timing to break through and from an African background it is expected that the oldest should marry before the youngest. We also see this in the story of Laban's daughters, when Jacob wanted to marry Rachel the youngest daughter and Laban told Jacob that it wasn't their custom to marry off a younger daughter ahead of the firstborn. Hence Jacob was deceived into marrying Leah. He worked a further seven years and eventually married Rachel who he loved. It makes it even harder for the oldest to get married, because everyone will see her as damaged goods.

Purpose doesn't give way to culture, traditions of men, first born, or last born. When it's your time, it's your time.

I had to embrace this level of understanding; but I also had to ensure that my own time would not pass me by.

I suppose you could say everything around me, my sister marrying before me, my younger brother's marrying before me and the flippant remarks from extended family members, was all working out for my good. It got me seeking God in Spirit and in Truth and He met me. I was no longer waiting in vain, but waiting in the Lord.

When I started walking in God's purpose for me, only then was I led into position, the place where my provision was.

What Does it Mean to Be in Position?
As a mentor, I have always told those who attend my classes that it is important to be in the right church. Let's face it, no church is perfect, as human beings we make mistakes, get it wrong, fall short of other's expectations of us, but as long as

you are based in the church that God wants you to be in, you will grow, and be fed with the appropriate food needed for your spiritual development. There is no point eating foods that will stunt your physical growth, why then eat spiritual food that will stunt your spiritual growth? God knows what you need and He sends you to the place you will get it.

The same applies to being in the right position to maximise your life performance. Why would I be with someone who will not enhance my life's purpose? This often happens when we're not in the right place at the right time.

Let's look at some of the prerequisites to being in position.

Your spirit, soul and body, must be in line with God's will

This means your spirit saved, soul renewed and discerning, and body prepared to do God's work in the place you're called to do it. Rebekah was at the well fetching water. You can argue that God led her there or she went there because she had a desire to fetch water, whatever the case she was in position, ready to serve. Furthermore, she had a beauty that caught the attention of the servant. Again it could be argued that she was naturally beautiful or the Spirit of God illuminated His beauty through her, it doesn't really matter. What counts is that she was where she was meant to be. She was in line with God's will for her life at that precise moment.

Another area that lets us down and prevents us being in position to receive is our emotions. Our emotions, if not managed, can delay and betray us. You cannot discern God's will through your emotions. If ninety-nine per cent of the time you have a feeling about something, most likely ninety-nine per cent of the time you can be wrong. Furthermore, if you made a decision on every emotion you had, most times your decision will be wrong. Your emotions, if not dealt with, can get in the way of

God's will for you.

When the servant told Rebekah's family that they would be leaving the following day—early morning, her family wanted her to stay behind for three more days; but she decided to go with Eliazar on the day he decided. If she made her decision on emotions and stayed back as her family requested, she may have missed her opportunity as Isaac's wife.

I remember a time when I was awoken in the very early hours of the morning to read a specific story in the bible or pray against certain barriers; little did I know that I was praying for my future, my husband and my children. My spirit was in line with God's will for me at that precise moment. I was being prepared to take a journey I had no idea about.

Did I want to continue my sleep in my comfortable bed? Yes! But needs are a must. You'll never miss out if you're in line and discern what He requires you to do at every given opportunity. Obedience is better than sacrifice.

Being in position doesn't mean you're comfortable. I wasn't comfortable waking up during the early hours to pray when others were enjoying the warmth of their beds, but it was given to me to do and I did it with all diligence.

It was given to Rebekah to follow Eliazar to meet Isaac on the day appointed and she went without hesitating.

Timing

I'm often asked when do you know it's time—to change jobs, move home, get married.

No one can tell you God's timing for you. Only you can discern when that is. What I do know is that He makes everything perfect in His timing; and the process we go through with Him is to understand how to discern the times and seasons we're in and what we should do to prepare in each season.

There was a time I had to fast, a time to pray/war, a time to worship, a time to praise. Each activity was bringing into manifestation His appointed time for me.

The truth is you are prepared by the activity you engage in. You are preparing for the next phase of your life and if that entails marriage then preparation will bring you to the appointed time.

The process to get you to the appointed time is strengthening your faith to do something that you wouldn't do in your own strength.

When we met, my husband told me that he believed he was also being prepared. From spending time on sets and hotels in between acting scenes, suddenly his whole life changed; activities in the movie environment was replaced with activities in the church. He moved homes, got involved in a prayer team where he would spend Friday all night in prayer, and he also enrolled in the worship ministry in his church. His priorities changed. The time he gained away from acting was replaced with church activities. This all happened before I was even thinking of travelling.

It seemed like all of a sudden God had us in our individual locations working to meet at His time. It wasn't about me or Frank, but about God preparing both of us for His perfect timing.

In that time His promise was tested, through the process of maturity to meet His perfect timing.

The right timing is important to take hold of God's provision. Even the bible says there is a time for everything. For everything there is a season, a time for every activity under heaven.

When your spirit, soul and body are in line with God's Spirit, you'll also be in tune with His timing and what is needed for you to get into position.

Location

Sometimes the place we're most comfortable is the place where we believe our needs are met. But more than likely, the most comfortable of places could be the farthest from our provision.

I was so convinced that England was where the Holy Spirit wanted me to be and surely the place where I would meet my husband, so I was so shocked when an assistant pastor of a church called me up one day while I was clothes shopping to tell me that she was praying that morning and felt led to call me to tell me to start praying about the location I should move to.

I was silent for a while and then asked her what she meant. She replied by telling me to go and enquire from the Holy Spirit.

When I started praying about my location and where the Holy Spirit wants me, I felt strongly in my spirit that God had been waiting for me to ask Him this question so that He could answer me.

Through praying I had a sense of leaving England. I saw myself flying overseas, so I certainly knew that I was meant to be going somewhere, but where was another question.

My whole mind was focused on relocation to America. I have close family based there and it wouldn't be too hard a process to relocate and find my feet.

But in the midst of processing my thoughts about America, I never in my wildest dreams thought that I would be going to Africa, in particular Nigeria.

I was at work one day and a close friend who later became a

mentee, spoke to me as if she had been part of my prayer to God; she said that she saw me going back to Nigeria and it was very soon.

She also added that she could see a queue of women waiting for me and for a long time I've had my back to them, but could now see that I was turning round to face them. I stupidly looked at her wondering what was she talking about. What does she know that I don't know? After a minute's silence she said, 'God is calling you back to Nigeria.'

My mouth fell open ready to drop to the ground. Surely she didn't know my prayers to God regarding my location and where He is sending me.

I realised that this woman was whom God had used to answer me. He was sending me to Nigeria!

Nigeria was a very unlikely place. How can God use me in Nigeria, it's been a very long time since I stepped foot in Nigeria; people are looking to come out of the country and yet here I was being sent to the country.

I had so many questions and no one to talk to. Everything made sense concerning the restlessness with my life, being stagnant, not having anymore grace to see me continue in the job I hated and the neighbourhood I was fed up with. It really made sense that God had more for me and I needed to go to the place to get it.

I would like to use this avenue to encourage you not to become too comfortable in your surroundings that you pass up whatever opportunity may connect you to your purpose.

There are some who are happy to stay where they are and believe whatever God has for them must be where they're already based and sometimes that's not always the case. We allow material possessions to keep us from following the Holy Spirit to the place our provision has prepared for us. As I was preparing to make my journey to Nigeria, I had to get rid of so much 'stuff' I had acquired over the years. I also had to take what was relevant to my move.

The more I threw away things I didn't need or gave to others, the more the grace overshadowed me to go to Nigeria. I didn't feel that I was carrying so much with me. To confirm this, I discerned the Holy Spirit say that material things are what keep people from following Him to their destiny.

We lay emphasis on the material things we have and as such they can present a barrier to moving to a new level, new environment or new lifestyle. We can be set in our ways and what the Holy Spirit requires of us is to follow Him. Our mind set is our enemy because when we hear the instruction which should be simple enough, we make it complicated because we start doubting or second guessing our hearing; I put this down to the 'stuff', the material possessions, that we own and hold dear to our hearts.

The same can be depicted in the form of the 'stuff' we carry in our hearts, how we can't flow due to spiritual weights we carry. In moving locations, it is important not to take things that you don't need, things that can't go where you're going; that could disrupt your journey.

I remember an instruction I had a few years before this actual season of my journey. I was told I should be ready to move, don't take old stuff, only take what He tells me to take, because on the way there will be a transference of wealth.

I now understand that I could only take what was needed for my journey; and everything I took was what was needed in Nigeria, even down to my diary, which held quite a few bits of important information that I would later need to use whilst out there. And there was a transference of wealth—I got married! And everything we needed for our wedding ceremony was already provided.

What I was saving up to get married in England was already provided for us in the location I was called to be married—Nigeria!

Walking in Obedience

It takes walking in obedience to instructions to obtain everything you need for the vision. As I stated earlier, provision is not limited to money, it can be whatever you need to fuel your vision. It could be favour, more time, opportunity, support etc.

Eliazar walked in obedience to Abraham's instructions and saw Rebekah at the well at the right time. Who knows if it was anyone else, she may not have bothered to give his camels water.

We are reminded in Isaiah 1:19, 'If you will only obey Me, you will have plenty to eat.'

What would it take for one to obey instructions that will get results?

Developing your faith in God and His Word— without faith it's impossible to please God; for they that come to Him must believe He is a Rewarder of those who diligently seek Him.

When you diligently seek God about something and He gives you a word, the word will be tested. The process you go through to hold onto the word and see the promise come to pass will definitely develop your faith.

In going to God for something, you are seeking Him, you have to believe that He will definitely reward you for what you're seeking Him for; it therefore requires you stick to everything you are told to do and do it whole heartedly. Obedience is key, it's better than sacrifice like the bible teaches.

My desire to be married and to see God fulfil it for me was what developed my faith. I held onto every word and instruction that was given to me.

Do what God tells you to do, even when it doesn't make sense to your own understanding.

Read some of the stories in the bible of people who did what they believed they were told to do, even when it didn't make sense, and see what successful results they received.

Most instructions given to us by God may not make sense to the human understanding and that's okay. It's not meant to make sense to someone that is not carrying the vision. You're carrying the vision so it's for you to follow God, and understanding comes after you've done what you're meant to do.

Every instruction God gives you has been seasoned with grace, so you're not alone doing it. He has empowered you with the grace to do it. Furthermore, His instructions, when carried out, comes with a blessing.

We are told to 'trust in the Lord with all our heart and lean not to our own understanding, in all our ways acknowledge Him and He will direct our path'.

In following God's instructions, you will have to leave some people behind, most times it will be those who have already labelled you and believe you've lost the 'plot'. My advice to you is to get on with whatever instructions you've been given and when you get to where you're going in your purpose, they'll see the achievements.

My family wasn't in agreement with me going to Nigeria, they actually thought I was having a nervous breakdown—going back to Nigeria? Are you out of your senses? But I knew that

I heard and I knew I had to go with what I heard. I had the peace and I had the grace.

Today, married with two beautiful girls is confirmation that I heard. I heard and I acted on what I heard even when it didn't make sense to me and those around me.

'And It Came to Pass' — Receive the Promise
The bible has many short, easy-to-remember phrases full of insight and spiritual advice. These phrases are even better when someone adds a twist to an ancient saying to make it relevant to modern life. We've all heard the biblical phrase 'And it came to pass'. You find this saying sprinkled liberally throughout the bible. Most of us think of this phrase as meaning 'and then it happened'.

Whatever has been promised to you will always be yours waiting for you to receive it. It requires your preparation according to His will, getting into the right location according to His will, acting on the right timing according to His will; all of this is seasoned with patience and in the fullness of time it will come to pass, it has to because it's a promise.

This promise was established for your life when you were conceived. Not now, not yesterday; but during the conception of your life, because it involves your purpose, and whoever God has called you to build with to fulfil His purpose on earth HAS TO COME TO PASS. It doesn't matter what wrong you've done, what lifestyle you've lived, as long as you get in line with the path to receive your promise, it will come to pass.

Promises bring hope, for example, there was God's promise to Abraham. Since there was no greater to swear by, God took an oath in His own name, saying:

> *'I will certainly bless you, and I will multiply your descendants beyond number.' Then Abraham waited patiently, and received what God*

had promised. (Hebrews 6:13—15)

Receiving is not hard when you've been obedient. Sometimes the trials we pass through can harden us, which can keep us in trials that should have been completed. We forget that every season must end for a new season to come in. Never get to the point where your trial has made you doubtful, discouraged or frustrated where you give up and forget that you have a blessing waiting for you at the end of it. If this is you, then open your heart and cry out to God to soften your heart, and continue with the instructions to receiving the promise.

I know many who've waited and waited expecting to meet their mates at a particular time and it didn't come as they expected. Then in getting tired sadly they've compromised.

It can happen to anyone, hence our reason to be vigilant.

I would like to encourage those of you who've waited and waited expecting to be married by a certain time in your life, not to lose hope. Be the best person for God that you can be whilst you are waiting, get on His path to preparation, not your path, but His. Whatever He wants to develop in you allow the development to be perfected by Him. I know He's heard your heart and is preparing you for that marriage partner.

He knows who He's called you to build with in purpose. Your waiting is not a mistake, it's for a purpose and it will come to pass.

For I know the plans I have for you says the Lord.
They are plans for good and not for disaster, to give a future and a hope.

Jeremiah 29:11

Reflection Time

- A strong reflection of your relationship with the Holy Spirit is required for you to answer the following questions:

- How has your life's process so far prepared you to be a wife/husband ready for a purpose-driven marriage?

- What areas in your life do you think you may be struggling with that could prevent a leading into position?

- What do you think if any, could be a barrier that is preventing you from seeing/receiving the marriage partner God has for you?

- Are there things that the Holy Spirit has put on your heart that you haven't done yet?

CHAPTER SEVEN

*The Purpose
Driven Marriage*

7

The Purpose Driven Marriage

As a single woman, my view of marriage was like someone looking at it through rose coloured glasses. There is nothing wrong with this, but it's very important to have in depth clarity about what marriage is all about. At the time my desire to meet a man, marry, have a companion and be 'in love' for the rest of our lives, outweighed what I thought a purpose driven marriage was all about. My single and carefree nature summed it up: all you need is love to be married.

Marriage is not just about people being in love, it's also not about two people having sex. If it were, then after the experience of a wonderful sexual fulfilment, what else can either of you bring to the table? If it were about being 'in love', what happens when you wake up one morning and the 'in love' experience with your husband or wife is not grabbing you. Do you make a choice to end the marriage? Life is not all about sex and being in love, there has to be something more fulfilling to bring a man and a woman together in marriage.

I enjoy all these experiences in my marriage, but I know there's a purpose for our marriage.

In developing my faith and my relationship with the Holy Spirit, I started to realise that marriage is not all about being in love with your spouse, but there is a greater purpose to marriage.

Being in love with someone is not enough to hold a marriage together. There are other qualities that a good marriage needs for it to survive, such as sacrifice, vision, support, provision, understanding, longsuffering, humility, accountability, patience, respect, most of all unconditional love (agape) and much more. A purpose driven marriage was not created to survive in isolation of these qualities but on the premise that all qualities are operational and working together. Such qualities will not operate in just any relationship, but a purpose driven marriage.

What is a Purpose Driven Marriage?

Where there is anything that's designed, there is a designer. Whether it's a truck, building or train—or even marriage—there is always a mastermind behind the masterpiece. God, the mastermind of marriage, also has a plan for how marriage works best.

It can be overwhelming to try and understand God's design and plan for marital love because contradicting and varying messages are everywhere: in books, magazines, movies and music. As a result, many couples fall into the trap of looking everywhere but to the Designer to find out what God intended for marriage. If you've tried understanding marriage through the world, there's a better way.

In Chapter One I mentioned that I attended a leadership conference where Dr Myles Munroe was the main speaker. His topic was based on relationships, in particular marriages, and he described marriage like that of an omelette. It's only as good as the eggs involved in making the omelette. If there is one good egg and one bad egg, it doesn't matter how good the one egg is, the omelette will still be rotten.

If the singles are contaminated, the marriage will naturally be contaminated. To understand this concept, it is important to go back to the beginning. But before going back, let's look at some brief statistics:

It's been forecasted that in the United Kingdom one out of every three marriages will end in divorce. In the United States of America it's presently recorded that one out of every two marriages will end in divorce. This tells us that the chances of a marriage actually working is fifty per cent, which means that for every five unions to go to the altar, 2.5 of them will end in tragedy (called divorce).

We are seeing this figure slowly seeping its way into the Christian community (the Church). Sadly we are dealing with an issue that the Church is very quiet about and the government doesn't know the answer to. The issue I'm talking about is relationships. Divorce is not only a major problem of the present, but it was also a problem 2000 years ago.

Is Divorce—A Problem or Symptom?
Moses was the first person to do something about marital legislation. He developed a bill of divorcement to prevent people from destroying each other.

When the Pharisees asked Jesus the question about a man divorcing a woman for any reason in Matthew 19:3, Jesus answered the question but ignored the issue, because He didn't see divorce as an issue but rather a symptom.

Divorce is a symptom that something is wrong in the relationship. For example, when there is a pain in the body, the pain is an indication that there is a problem. Our body was created by God to be such a unique machine, that whenever something is wrong with our bodies, the neurological system will communicate to our brain that something is wrong somewhere. The neurological impulses will send a signal of that problem to the brain; and the brain will then send a signal back to that area to inform that area to emit a signal that there is something wrong.

The signal that the area emits is called pain, so when you feel pain, that pain is not the problem. Therefore, the pain is the neurological system telling our bodies that something is wrong in that location and so we can act and deal with the problem.

Divorce works in the same way. The fact that there are so many problems in families, disintegrating marriages and broken homes is not the problem; the problem is that something else is wrong and divorce is the symptom of the problem, that's why divorce is so painful. Divorce is worse than death. When one dies, there is a funeral, a ceremony to say good-bye – then there's closure.

On the other hand, divorce is the death of a marriage, you walk away from the life you had with this person. There is no burial of the people involved, only the relationship. There will be times when you see each other with other partners, or one may keep coming back. It's a kind of death, but no closure especially if children are involved. And that in itself can be painful.

That's why God says He hates divorce!

When the Pharisees asked Jesus a question about divorce, He answered:

> *'Haven't you heard the scriptures? It is recorded that from the beginning God made them male and female. And He said, this explains why a man leaves his father and mother and is joined to his wife, and the two are united into one. Since they are no longer two, but one, therefore let no one split apart what God has joined together.'* (Matthew 19:4-6 NLT).

The man and woman that God joins together are those who qualify in the verse: 'It is recorded that from the beginning God made them male and female, therefore let no one split apart what God has joined together'. No one should split apart the two that God has joined together.

Which is why divorce is not the problem; the problem is who has been joined together. The community, the government, the world is not joining together who God joins together.

In the beginning it wasn't so, that's why Jesus didn't see it as a problem, He referred the Pharisees back to the beginning: 'Haven't you heard the scriptures? It is recorded that from the beginning...'

The First Male and Female

God only created one human being from the soil (Genesis 2:7); He never went back. Today we have over five billion people, but the first person God made was male.

It's important to note that when building anything, the foundation must first be laid; after the foundation is laid it's hidden because it's underneath the building. The foundation is the most important part of the building because it holds the entire structure and carries the weight of everything. This means that the foundation must be given a lot of attention.

Contractors will tell you that more money goes into the foundation than the whole building. This will involve digging to bedrock, then laying steel, mortar and concrete. They reinforce it and build the foundation based on the entire weight of the structure, including the furniture, the people, the decorations.

In other words, an engineer will calculate the weight of the building before he will give the specifications for the foundation.

d began the human family, He calculated everything
uld take to carry the weight of the human family and
nclusion was that He would construct a foundation and
t 'Male'.

The First True Male Man

The first male was built to carry the weight of the family. Most men are not aware of this, so they run from the weight of the responsibility. Every male was designed by God to carry the entire weight of their family. If a man has 10 children, he was built to carry that family.

To understand this is to understand God the Father. Whatever comes out of something sustains it; that's where the word father comes from. Father means source, sustainer; the male came from God. God created the male from Himself. The male source is God Himself; this means God is the Father of the male.

On the other hand, the first female, Eve didn't come from the soil, she came from the male (Genesis 2:21—22), hence the male is the father of the female. In other words, the male came from God and the female came from the male.

When Jesus said: 'Haven't you heard the scriptures? It is recorded that from the beginning God made them male and female.'

He meant to have a good marriage, you have to go back to the beginning; therefore divorce is not the problem but the material used for the marriage may not have the right criteria. Study what a male and female were like in the beginning, and once you can find that these two qualify by that criteria, then that marriage will work.

A man and a woman cannot get a divorce unless they're married and they can't get married unless they're two individuals.

And the process to this starts with God producing a male; the male produces a female and when the two come together, they produce a marriage. So the two have to be of the right ingredients to form a purpose driven marriage, the basis for a solid family unit.

Qualities of the First True Male Man

Clear Self Image—he knew he was the image of God. Such a man is not trying to be like other people, he doesn't need anyone's approval to feel important, to dress like others, speak like others. He is his own man who knows he's created in the image of God. He's self confidence is in God, not in any style or in any role model somewhere else.

He was placed in the Garden of Eden— a true male when you meet him is in the Presence of God.

- His first command was work—such a man when you meet him is working and loves to work.

- He was instructed to cultivate—which means a true male can cultivate his woman. To cultivate her means to bring the best out of her, so he will increase, improve her value, advance and develop her.

- God told the man to guard the Garden— that means a true male is a protector; he will not abuse, violate or harass his wife and children. He protects everything under his care.

- He was given the first command (Genesis 2:17) – the true male knows the Word and the commandments of God and feeds it to his family.

When God said, 'It is not good for the man to be alone', He was referring to the men who have the characteristics of the first true male man.

The First True Female Woman
'So the Lord God caused the man to fall into a deep sleep. While the man slept, the Lord God took out one of the man's ribs (one of his sides) and closed up the opening. Then the Lord God made a woman from the rib (his side).'

In actual fact, God goes into the real man and makes another man and built this one with a womb – this man was called a womb-man. He took this womb-man and presented her to Adam. God did not make Adam a wife, but a helper to help him carry out his dominion responsibilities. It was Adam who spotted this womb-man and said: This is bone from my bone (structure), and flesh from my flesh! No hairs on her skin like the animals, and she is upright. She will be called 'woman', because she was taken from me.

Just as Adam called and named the animals, he named the womb-man. God didn't name her, Adam did.

Adam also prophesied that because woman was produced from man, for this reason a man will leave his father and mother and join to his wife, because she was taken from him and the two become one. Provided it's a female who possesses the ingredients of the first true female woman, he will leave his Father God and cleave to her. Don't forget, Adam was in the Garden working, cultivating, protecting in God's Presence, but when he saw Eve he was prepared to leave and cleave. It's part of God's order; and His order flows when everything's in place.

God is the Father of the male; male is the father of the female and when they both come together it produces a marriage provided they are of the right ingredients.

What kind of female was produced from Adam?
The man is a spirit; the woman is also a spirit. The man has no gender because he's a spirit; the woman has no gender because she's also a spirit. The man is eternal; the woman is also eter-

nal. The man has the Glory of God; the woman also has the Glory of God. The man has the nature of God; the woman has the nature of God. Spiritually they are both equal. However, in order for them to complement each other and build a purpose driven marriage, there are principle differences.

Eve met Adam in Eden; Adam was the first person presented in the Garden, Eve was the second in the Garden. She met Adam in the Presence of the Lord. Single women should always marry a man who they meet in the Presence of the Lord. It goes against God's order or a purpose driven marriage to find a man outside the Presence of the Lord and bring him into the Presence of the Lord.

The male was given work first; she was created to help him work. Adam was given the word/instruction first, although she wasn't given the word directly, she was supposed to be the recipient of the word from the male. He was given an assignment first and she was assigned to dominate with him.

Qualities of the First True Female Woman
The male is the responsible head; head doesn't mean better, it means responsible. The female was sent to help him; she is a helper. The male is the source (provider); the female is the incubator. The male is a cultivator; the female is supposed to be the producer. He is the giver and the female is supposed to be the receiver. He is the protector and she is supposed to be the encourager. He is the developer and the female is supposed to be the nurturer. The male is a source, a teacher, and the female is supposed to be the resource (give commands) after she's learned from her husband. He is the teacher; but she is the prophetess (encourages, edifies and empowers with God's Word).

The female is an incubator; she gives life to everything. As a prophetess she receives, expands and gives it back but never in the same way she received it. It is always given back multiplied.

As an encourager, when her man shares his dreams, she needs to encourage him even when it seems impossible.

As women we want whatever we desire. However a female who has the ingredients of the first female woman would not put her husband under undue pressure to go and get whatever she sees and wants.

As a prophetess, she receives information, expands it and gives it back multiplied. Therefore, a male must have a plan ready for his woman to help him. A woman comes loaded; she has the equipment (intelligence, intuition, wisdom, insight, sensitivity, power, incubation, anointing) ready to help. However, the female's role is never to usurp authority over the male because she may be initially more equipped than he is; she is to use her resources to help him achieve his vision.

The Holy Spirit is called the same thing a woman is called too. Jesus said the Holy Spirit is a Confidant, hence He never comes to take over our lives, but to help us do what we're doing. If we don't plan, we have given the Holy Spirit nothing to do.

The female 'man' is a wise woman; she builds her house with her hands and refrains from tearing it down with her mouth.

When a woman comes to a man with her vision and doesn't submit to his vision, that opens an opportunity for divorce.

A female 'man' studies her husband, asks him questions to find out what his dream/vision/desire is.

As a helper, you can't help someone whose assignment you don't know. Even if he isn't the ideal man right now, to build a purpose driven marriage, your role is to help him become that. A helper is someone who will always assist.

God's Model Design for
The Purpose Driven Marriage

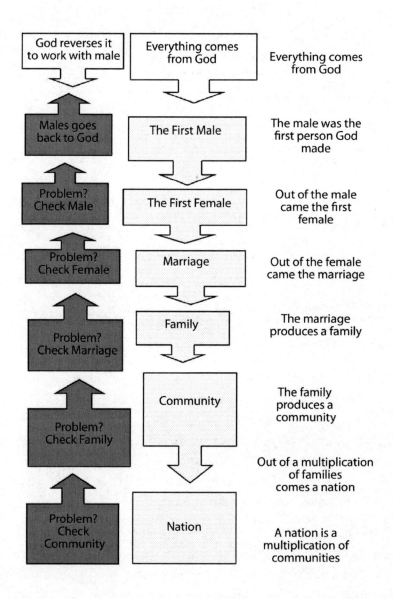

God reverses it to work with male	Everything comes from God	Everything comes from God
Males goes back to God	The First Male	The male was the first person God made
Problem? Check Male	The First Female	Out of the male came the first female
Problem? Check Female	Marriage	Out of the female came the marriage
Problem? Check Marriage	Family	The marriage produces a family
Problem? Check Family	Community	The family produces a community
		Out of a multiplication of families comes a nation
Problem? Check Community	Nation	A nation is a multiplication of communities

Whenever there's a problem in the nation, such as promiscuity or divorce, you've got to go backwards to find the problem.

Check the community for the problem. If it's the community, then something must be wrong with the family, if it's the family, then something must be wrong with the marriage, if the marriage, then something must be wrong with the woman. If there is something wrong with the woman, then something must be wrong with the man.

The man goes back to God and then God reverses it to the man and works with him to find out where the problem is. The solutions starts with the man.

God teaches the man by turning the hearts of the fathers back to the children.

A woman is as good as the man cultivates her; marriages are as good as the male and females that are in it.

If the singles are contaminated, a marriage will naturally be contaminated. Therefore it is important to check the male and female first before God is blamed.

To have and accomplish a purpose driven marriage, there is a need to check the quality of people that make up the marriage because your marriage will only be as good as the singles; there is a need to build together and it takes time to invest into a life long union. There is a need to be responsible in your roles as husband, wife and parents and then being accountable to each other and to God will not be such a challenge.

Being single and what you do as a single person, is more important than marriage because your marriage will only be good as your singleness. When your heart is given to God, you submit to His molding you into the female woman that was produced from the male man, ready for a purpose driven marriage.

And if you want your marriage to improve, you don't ask your mate to improve, you improve and it will automatically improve your marriage because it's designed on God's order of a purpose driven marriage and you are your marriage.

Your spouse, when you find him or her, should be as close as possible to the beginning man and woman and this is God's will for a Purpose Driven Marriage.

The Art of Marital Bliss

So here I am. I remember laying on my bed in 1998 crying to God asking Him when will I ever be married.

I didn't think to ask will I be married, just when. I assumed that everyone who desires to be married will be married someday and I was no exception.

I imagined myself walking down the aisle to meet the man of my dreams and everything, absolutely everything would be wonderful. This man I was waiting for will look after me from now on and all my problems will be over.

It's 2011, I've been married for five years, with two beautiful girls; ask me whether I am happy. Am I enjoying married life? Am I loving being a wife, a mother and having to build a ministry, business and continue writing my books?

Am I enjoying marital bliss?

This morning, my husband leaves early for work. I decide it's too early to get up so I go back to bed. Before I do, I listen out for the girls in their bedroom and I can't hear the sound of an early morning sing song, the rattling of toys, the little competitive arguments as to who wants to make pretend tea for their stuffed dolls. I decide another hour of uninterrupted sleep won't hurt.

But before I close my eyes to sheer peace, I hear a text come through on my phone. I open it up and it reads: 'Thanks so much sweetheart. I really am blessed to have you as a wife. You are a genius and a role model.'

Yes, it's from my husband. Before he set off to work, he sent me this text. Did I do anything at that moment to deserve this? No. Was I expecting it? No. Did it make me smile? Yes.

Being married to the person I was meant to marry is what counts. We have our ups and downs, our terrible arguments, waiting for the other to apologise. But all in all, I can say that his approach to our marriage has allowed me to be me, to develop my gifts and utilise my creativity, and in doing so, I am growing everyday in my role as a wife and mother.

When I got married, my problems didn't go away. He swept me off my feet but not into the moonlight to live happily ever after. He definitely is the man for me, not a fairy tale character.

And finally, I wouldn't say I know it all in marriage. I still have a lot to learn, but then life is all about learning and if I knew it all, then maybe I wouldn't have written this book.

I married God's best for me and we're making it work, and that is the art of marital bliss.

Unless the Lord builds a house,
The work of the builder is wasted.
Unless the Lord Protects a city,
guarding it with sentries will do no good.
It is useless for you to work so hard
from early morning until late at night
anxiously working for food to eat;
for God gives rest to his loved ones.

Psalm 127: 1–2 NLT

Reflection Time

- In reflecting on the First Male Man and Female Woman, how does your qualities and character line up with their qualities and character?

- Are you or someone else that you know of experiencing marital issues that God's Model Design for a Purpose Driven Marriage could help?

- What areas of the design are applicable to you and how can they be resolved?

Author's Conclusion

Do you or someone you know need restoration in their marriage? Perhaps you may know of a single man or woman who has been waiting, hoping, desiring to experience the married life and is tired of the waiting game.

The truth is there are so many books and seminars on marriage and relationships out there; however, no one has the answer but the person who created the institution in the first place.

This book has been written from my burning desire in wanting to be married and my passion in waiting on God to do it His Way—and He did.

Every piece of information that you may find that will help you, as long as it's based on the TRUTH and your inner convictions, when applied will bring you one step closer to your vision.

What you need is an inner strong conviction that God's promises for your life will come to pass. When it does I don't know, but I know it will come to pass.

Mary asked the angel, Gabriel, 'How could this be?' when she was given the prophecy. She believed God could do what He said He would do, but it's in my opinion that I don't think she believed that it could be done through her as she pondered on the message.

God created the institution of marriage. That means it would seem right to go back to Him to ask Him for His plan for you to enter into that institution. When you do as and what He says, you will be the one to declare your testimony.

So going back to my first question, about who you know that may need something to encourage them along their wait or in their trial in this area, if this book has empowered you in the area you needed it to, and you believe it will with others, then don't hold back – bless them and wait for your time to come to pass too.

Be Empowered!

Jacqueline Nwokeji-Ani